Raising Multicultural Awareness in Higher Education

Ana Maria Klein

UNIVERSITY PRESS OF AMERICA,® INC.
Lanham • Boulder • New York • Toronto • Oxford

Copyright © 2006 by
University Press of America,® Inc.
4501 Forbes Boulevard
Suite 200
Lanham, Maryland 20706
UPA Acquisitions Department (301) 459-3366

PO Box 317
Oxford
OX2 9RU, UK

Library of Congress Control Number: 2005928416
ISBN 0-7618-2886-9 (paperback : alk. ppr.)

∞™ The paper used in this publication meets the minimum
requirements of American National Standard for Information
Sciences—Permanence of Paper for Printed Library Materials,
ANSI Z39.48—1992

DEDICATION

I dedicate this book to all of my students. I have been raising cultural awareness for almost four years now and get very excited about how they inform me with their thoughts and ideas. Each semester, as I prepare my course syllabi, I am energized with their suggestions. Whenever I choose a topic to write about, I am enriched with their heartfelt responses to the activities we do in class together. I thrive on their energy.

This is the reason I have put together this book, to work with them and to communicate with them in a more personal and transparent fashion.

I would also like to dedicate this book to the wonderful faculty of the College of Education at SUNY Fredonia who have trusted me and encouraged me for the past five years. It is a real pleasure to work with such an uplifting team of people. We share a lot of the preparing, planning and instructing tasks that make ours such a great program.

My professors and advisors at McGill University in Montreal deserve a heartfelt thank you as they shaped my ideas and thoughts throughout my doctoral studies (1996–1999).

Experiencing my own awakening and cultural journey after uprooting from my native Venezuela helped shape my own approach to developing a keen sensitivity towards cultural differences. For this, I thank my husband and children. They supported me, rooted for me and provided me with a safe haven of love and understanding when I most needed it.

Contents

Contents

Foreword

The increasing diversity that defines American institutions in the 21st century calls for a new approach on the part of teachers in order to prepare the new crop of a more diversified generation of students to appreciate and participate effectively in the American dream. However, the truism is that while America's public schools are undergoing a dramatic shift that reflects the growing diversity of the population, many educators and the schools in which they work seem no better prepared for this change. Thus, it is not surprising that raising multicultural awareness has become a perennial theme of intense interest to American educators. Many conferences, seminars and workshops have been organized at national and international levels through which many educators and researchers have articulated the need to keep abreast of diversity issues in academia.

Thus, *Raising Multicultural Awareness in Higher Education* has not come more at a better time as it provides a comprehensive resource and activities to assist students and teachers in universities, colleges, and research institutions among others, in understanding diversity as a key issue in academia today. Thus the book serves as an insightful portrait of one of the most talked about educational issues, as it is thought-provoking, inspiring and informative. It is practical and down to earth, yet full of exhaustive academic work as evidenced by the copious activities found at the end of each chapter. The book will find application in colleges, libraries, and school programs as it serves as an invaluable resource to refresh the spirit of all educators who are committed to reaching every student in their classrooms. No doubt it opens a new frontier of scholarly exploration as

the content and thought expressed in the book will significantly contribute
to diversity issues in higher education in the years ahead.

Dr. Lewis Asimeng-Boahene
Assistant Professor of
Social Studies Education
Department of Education
Penn State Harrisburg

Preface

This book is written for pre-service teachers, teacher-candidates, and teaching enthusiasts who believe in becoming aware and informed *reflective practitioners* in their future classrooms. The author, an assistant professor at a state university, shares her teaching and learning experiences in a manageable and research-informed forum throughout the textbook.

Divided into fifteen chapters, the book follows an organic exploration of theory, practice and personal reflection. The format includes exercises designed for readers to begin to develop and enhance their sense of self. In so doing, readers also develop and enhance their awareness of others.

The individual chapters of the textbook are broken down into three parts, (1) Theory (2) Practical Applications and (3) Reflections. These three distinct units evolve as explorations of (1) Self and Other (2) Teaching and Learning and (3) Reflections from the field. As readers explore the contents of the textbook, and carry out the suggested teaching and learning exercises, they will find themselves equipped with a toolkit for addressing *Multicultural Education* concerns.

Carlos Diaz, in his book *Multicultural Education for the 21st Century*, reminds us that seasoned educators (those from my generation 1950–1970's) were not taught Multicultural Educational ideas as a canon or discipline. In other words, educators like me were not trained to teach in the diversely populated school environments we find today. Aside from not having had a forum for discussion of salient issues regarding cultural and linguistic diversity, we weren't given the kinds of management and instructional tools needed to handle these issues in our classrooms. Today, we are required to put into practice equitable learning environments which include all learners. We need to be well trained ourselves and to serve as examples and role models for colleagues, administrators and our entire student body. Because the equity principle and the

No Child Left Behind Act did not affect our teaching back then in my day, it is important to be informed about how it affects all of us today, seasoned, novice and experienced teachers alike. In my experience as a classroom generalist for over twenty-five years, I can vouch for myself and my devoted colleagues. We did what we could to teach fairly. Yet, we were not informed about all of the adaptations, modifications and services we have available to us to spread the learning more evenly.

As we begin to do what we've learned to do in the college classroom, and to integrate a multicultural perspective into our daily teaching endeavors, we might not be well received by experienced and seasoned teachers who haven't had the kinds of training we've had. We might ultimately experience resistance and other not too exciting reactions to the decisions we make and the types of teaching we embrace. I hope this toolkit is a handy instrument for you as you continue to embrace a multicultural way of teaching.

PART ONE SELF AND OTHER

Chapter one deals with a visceral exploration of self as a social individual. As we read the chapter and do the exercises, we begin to air and disclose certain things about ourselves that define us as cultural beings. We learn about how our own identities were formed, we discover which groups we side or align with, and begin to understand the *Goals of Multicultural Education* (Banks, 2003). Re-viewing a classic film collectively and responding to a question-naire allows readers to revisit their personal biases.

Chapter two deals with *identity-formation*. We explore our cultural identi-ties and those of our students. As we start exploring how a deep understanding of self leads to a strong identity-building foundation, we begin to embrace the *equity principle* and to teach all students so that in fact *no child is left behind*.

We explore our own biases and impediments that could have sent strong negative messages to our peers and students. In doing so, we talk about the *Deficit Model/Deficit Orientation* (Banks, 2003.) We also explore the term *ethnocentrism* and how it affects our teaching. We then start to explore the history of how *multicultural education* was excluded from the curriculum.

Based on the ideas of equitable educational opportunities for all learners, we focus on student-centered instruction. This leads us to move from focus-ing on teaching and the teacher towards focusing on the pupil/student and learner. We analyze teaching and learning styles to better understand the fil-ters and channels necessary for providing instruction in a safe classroom en-vironment. In so doing, we also explore the concept of a safe, equitable, em-pathetic and nurturing classroom environment. *Re-reading a classic book* and responding to it with our newly found multicultural lens is an activity that accompanies this chapter.

Chapter three focuses on the teacher and the concept of *cultural capital* and teacher as *cultural broker*. As we weave in the *multicultural teaching* and learning scenarios, we begin to explore the behavior of people within their different social groups. Identity formation, cultural awareness, and integration of the socially constructed facets of life are woven into our *multicultural education* goals. *Readers analyze a cultural group collectively.*

Chapter four focuses on teacher as *negotiator, change-agent,* and *peace-builder*. Classroom management and instructional ideas and suggestions are presented in detail. Pre-service teachers at this point are ready to enter the field. As they begin to do so, they are given opportunities to observe what goes on in a real classroom. They are also encouraged to keep a reflective journal to document classroom realities and to plan for their classrooms of the future. *The learning center* as an instructional tool is explored.

Chapter five explores the goals of teaching and learning in detail. *The ideal classroom* is designed to project the types of teaching and learning that will occur in our future classrooms. Classroom management principles are discussed as well as student engagement. *Readers experience self-regulated learning.*

PART TWO TEACHING & LEARNING

Chapter six introduces instructional ideas that connect and integrate learning. The thematic unit, lesson plans, rubrics and pre and post teaching activities are explored in great depth. *Readers create a draft thematic unit of their own.*

Chapter seven focuses on the engaged student and what he/she is encouraged to do in a multicultural classroom. Action research, data-informed learning, evidence-based instruction and the use of *realia* to enhance learning are explored. *Readers explore individualized instruction.*

Chapter eight focuses on James Banks' transformation model. Course participants have explored self and other as well as instructional scenarios. They have also spent time in a real classroom. At this point in time, mid-semester, they should also be experiencing some form of transformation. Readers explore the concept of teacher as broker, negotiator, informer and change agent. Readers *role play.*

Chapter nine concentrates on the three e's; empathy, equity and excellence. Legislation, the legacies of *Brown vs. Board* and *Lau vs. Nichols* as well as the mandates of the *No Child Left Behind Act* are put in a multicultural perspective. *Readers re-enact some of these court cases.*

Chapter ten recaptures the essence of multicultural education in light of the personal transformation, teaching and learning styles, information and the mission we have ahead of us. *Readers generate their own goals for multicultural education in their future classrooms.*

PART THREE REFLECTIONS

Chapter eleven explores the concept of life-long learner, providing participants with information and tools for engaging in extended learning. Cultural icons, elements of popular culture that shape our thinking and contemporary issues are related to the goals of *multicultural education. Readers explore popular culture and its effects on teaching and learning.*

Chapter twelve is a shared dialogue with multicultural educators and their constraints in the classroom.

Chapter thirteen offers a blueprint for the well-designed thematic unit. Several units are critiqued and improved. Ways of multiculturalizing instruction are shared.

Chapter fourteen celebrates our progress and assists us in moving forward. We discuss curricular constraints, the effect of standardized testing agendas in our teaching and administrative hurdles we might encounter. As the well-informed, socially aware change agents that we have become, we generate strategies for dealing with these issues multiculturally. Readers generate a school-wide *multicultural reform agenda.*

Chapter fifteen culminates our journey, celebrating our transformation and empowering us to continue doing what we already do so well. Readers reflect back and generate their own *"Magna Carta"* or *"Bill of Rights"* for multicultural education to flourish in their classrooms.

Chapter One

An Exploration of Self

This chapter deals with a *visceral* exploration of ourselves, as we become the social individuals that we are. As we read the chapter and do the exercises, we begin to air and disclose certain things about ourselves that define us as cultural beings. We learn about how our own identities were formed, we discover which groups we side or align with, and we begin to understand the *Goals of Multicultural Education* (Banks, 2003). As a shared exercise, we will review a classic film collectively, and respond to a questionnaire. This will allow both our readers and their professor to explore their own biases.

THEORIES ON DISCRIMINATION

In the course that I currently teach (Cultural & Linguistic Diversity) my students are shocked as they discover that racial *identity formation* is set at an early age, 2 or 3 years (Coles, 1992). They listen in disbelief as I describe the work of researchers (Allport, 1954, Coles, 1992; Paley, 1992) and other prominent authors who have observed young children at play. These authors explain how it is that children discriminate against others. In order for teachers to create a caring-centered, socially just teaching atmosphere for their students, they need to understand the nature of *caring* and *social justice*. As well, pre-service teachers, in-service teachers, and educational enthusiasts alike should begin to understand the reasons why discrimination and intolerance exist.

Let's begin to understand this concept by exploring it from its early roots. The early stages of rejection start during our early childhood (Paley, 2002). Vivian Paley's book (1992) *You Can't Say You Can't Play* brings out many cultural issues that surface during free time and during play among children. As she observes kindergartners at play, Paley says that when play is initiated

1

and defined by the key players, in this sense, children, some children will seek to gain power over others. This process defines the roles and hierarchies early on. These positions of power become permanent unless a consciously aware adult intervenes. She describes her intervention as one where institutes the disposition whereby nobody can exclude or reject anybody else in her classroom or in her playground. The book delightfully describes how Paley uses simulations, puppets, and toys to deliver her point.

I find it interesting that we need to model appropriate, socially appropriate, and classroom-safe behavior. I used to think that children were well intentioned, well meaning, and loving. What an eye-opener! I now understand the role of fables and tales. I used to think they were written for entertainment and never focused much on the moral of the stories. Now I realize they were written to explain, through story, what socially appropriate behaviors should be. If this is so, then what do we do to intervene when situations get out of control and aren't in our direct playground, our classrooms, or our line of supervision? My colleagues in multicultural education continue to remind me of our role as educators in a holistic sense. We need to put our foot down, to disseminate the word, and to promote equitable educational practices and learning environments for everybody and at all times. But, are we forgetting to draw the line when it comes to controlling/monitoring the negatively intended behavior youngsters express towards each other?

Allport (1954) describes prejudicial behavior as progressing in five stages. He says that if the behavior is not curtailed in one stage, it will evolve into the following stage. In other words, bad behavior, if not curbed, will snowball into worse behavior. These are the progressive stages that could be avoided with adequate intervention:

ANTILOCUTION

This type of behavior begins with name-calling. Children do it all the time. They probably learn it at home or in informal environments as a result of our society's competitive nature. It is not infrequent that we hear our own families siding with one football or baseball team and calling members of the other team all sorts of derogatory names. Children also capture these behaviors from our very own popular culture where bullies victimize or oppress weaker individuals. I could list many of these instances for you, but I'll let you do that on your own as you do the practice exercises at the end of the chapter.

Antilocution, as I see it, involves a reaffirmation of a powerful entity that has total control of a person or group. The oppressor or victimizer uses oppressive language or a code of language and behavior to curtail the rights of others. In children's behavior, it translates into formation of groups or cliques and an organized effort to exclude others. Allow me to illustrate. While doing classroom research during my doctoral studies, I witnessed something that I consider *antilocution* and that I have entitled the *whipping corner*. I have been a fourth-grade teacher for over twenty years. Hence, I bring a lot of personal experience into the judgment I'm going to make. At the time, I was observing a fifth-grade classroom, which in my experience matched my own fourth grade in another country. The sessions I observed were extended (90 minute) mathematical problem-solving lessons where students had a chance to work in groups, to walk around freely and to leave the room on their own if they needed to. At this point in time, I began to observe how a few girls always gravitated to the same corner of the room for extended periods of time. I thought they were heading back to their cubbies to retrieve a book, a folder, or some other personal item. However, I caught them heading back to this corner in small groups of three. As they headed back, a jolly two-some triumphantly embraced while the third girl was excluded and in distress. As I observed this pattern over and over again, I realized that the pair of girls, always the same ones, would call on another girl to take her to the corner to proceed to tell her off. The interactions that I heard were hateful, derogatory comments about whether the third girl had been loyal to them, etc. This sort of behavior should not happen and teachers should not allow more than one person to convene in such a "private" spot in the classroom.

AVOIDANCE

This means ignoring that the behavior happened. I see avoidance as happening in two directions, among the key players (the children) and their care providers (teachers, parents, peers, and older siblings). Avoidance becomes a bipartisan game, where one group rejects or avoids another and where people side against each other in a relational manner. *Avoidance* also becomes an adult defensive reaction whereby when there is a misbehavior the teacher doesn't see it or refuses to acknowledge it.

In my own experience, if I happened to detect something about a particular child or group of children, it wouldn't surprise me that other teachers would say: "Oh, he's good in my class and doesn't do that." Or, "I don't know what kind of rules you have in your classroom, but in mine, these things don't happen and they shouldn't be happening in yours." I've also heard this: "Oh, you know how girls are they're particular and cliquey anyway, so why intervene." So, once I've realized that teachers get defensive when it comes to discussing students we have in common, I understand this as an *avoidance mechanism*.

Let me share what happened after I observed the *whipping corner*. I reported this behavior to the teacher. She clearly understood what was going on, yet in disbelief, told me that research indicates that girls that age like to play in quiet places. To me, this was absolute avoidance of the problem and a total negation that there was a problem.

DISCRIMINATION

Discrimination is unfair treatment of others in every sense of the word. *Discrimination* is also the first realization that there is a difference. Scenes from my childhood appear as I recall what it was like to be discriminated against. Personally, I was the only freckled redhead in my class. Growing up in Venezuela, a Spanish-speaking country where everybody else came from a Hispanic background was not easy. Being Jewish didn't help either as most of my classmates were Catholic. I have a not so fond memory of not being allowed to enter a friend's home because of this. Scenes from books I've read and movies I've seen also pop up in my head as I recall discriminatory behavior.

For example in Graham Greene's short story *All in a Day*, the story takes place in an imaginary planet where it rains everyday and all of the time except for one day. The entire planet looks forward to this dry day. A group of children lock up one of their classmates so she can't experience the dry day. This to me is *discrimination* in the hands of children. Another scene that I remember is one from William Golding's *Lord of the Flies* where the children side with the leader and begin to discriminate against the weaker children. Actually, the book deals with all of Allport's levels, and I'll let you decipher them in the exercise at the end of the chapter.

PHYSICAL ATTACK

Physical Attack is a part of the progression of these painful events. If the behavior isn't curtailed in time, then events lead to this kind of violence. Teachers might not witness physical attack within the classroom walls as much as on the playground. Unfortunately, playground duty is often in the hands of paraprofessionals or teaching assistants who do not have other kinds of contact with the children.

I advise every teacher who prides him/herself as a well-rounded, well-informed, caring educator, to spend some time in the playground, because that's where they will perhaps discover and uncover who the bullies and victimizers are.

GENOCIDE

This would be that horrible last stage where the violence culminates in loss of life. Unfortunately, with the school shootings that we have witnessed over the past ten years, these things do happen. I often find myself discussing these events in class with my students. We come to the same realization, somebody knew about it before it even happened and never bothered to stop it. Why? Are we so afraid of each other that we are unwilling to help each other out?

We certainly don't expect young children to experience the latter two behaviors, attributing these to different situations. However, it is not unusual to encounter the first three behaviors in the classroom and on the playground. We could all conjure examples from our own experience. The point we need to make here is to introduce ways to deal with these types of behaviors.

Discrimination is taught and caught. This is quite a statement, isn't it? But, it reaffirms the fact that children learn discriminatory behaviors from their parents, siblings, teachers, and peers. Children notice differences. They compare themselves to other children and immediately notice hair and skin color as well as size, tone of voice, personality, and intentions. They also ask lots of questions. Usually, they seek reassurance and stability. I would say that most of the time children want to be safe and to feel safe. When they notice differences, they want to know how these differences actually affect them.

Children learn to act on these differences too. Sometimes they separate themselves from those they discriminate against and exclude others who do not have similar distinctive features or affiliations. We should be able to teach them to handle these behaviors fairly. We should also encourage children to look out for each other's safety. Let's not forget that children in our care spend a lot of time with us and respond to what we teach them. So, let's establish tolerance building in our daily classroom exercises, out in the playground, and in everything we do around young children.

Readers would be surprised at how much discriminatory behavior is handed down to us from previous generations. Just look at the proverbial fairy tales that were read to us as bedside stories. How much discriminatory activity is embedded within those texts? I ask you to recall some of these at the end of the chapter.

We spend many hours with youngsters in our classrooms. It is our job to help them feel safe so that they are free to learn, which is why they come to school. I urge teachers to think about ways they can teach youngsters peace-building activities so that none of Allport's levels arise in our classrooms. Good behaviors are taught and caught if children are encouraged to analyze what is going on and to make sense of the world. If we talk to them and speak with them clearly, I'm sure, they'll catch on and learn that it doesn't feel good to call people names, or to ignore people, and let's not progress to the more physical means of injustice.

THEORIES ON MULTICULTURAL EDUCATION

Our next question (now that we have leveled the teaching terrain and created a safe learning environment) is how do we import equity into our classrooms? How do we set up an environment where children can speak up and speak out equitably? What are some peer-mediated activities and classroom rules that we can implement?

I encourage you now, as you read this chapter, to reach back into your own playground experiences, to start remembering instances where you were treated unfairly or where you treated others unjustly. Let's purge all of this rejection you endured or had others endure. In this very visceral exercise, you need to be confronted with your own meanness to understand that human beings pursue power and control over any other goal.

Reaching back into our classroom experiences, I would also like to remind you that many forms of intolerance and discrimination are taught in our classrooms. We probably learned to reject certain people, cultural groups, or national groups right in school, through the ways history was taught to us. Let me give you an example. When I was in school, I remember learning to hate the lobster-backs or English soldiers that fought during the Revolutionary War. The way the teacher and our textbook presented these was like, here's this team and here's the other. We side with one and hate the other. I remember quoting my teacher often as I described the historic events in grade four.

James Loewen, (2001) in his book *Lies My Teacher Told Me* explores many of these historical narratives taught as misconceptions and ingrained in our collective consciences. Let's look, for example, at the story of Thanksgiving or the story of Columbus' exploration of the Americas. Students are entitled to know the truth about these events. Teachers should not continue promoting the same scenarios that were conveniently taught to them. Thanksgiving should be taught as a lesson on sharing. Columbus' exploration should be taught as the uncovering of the Americas and as a geography lesson where students should be engaged in the real skills of measuring location and calculating distance.

At this point in time, I'd like to address the *Goals of Multicultural Education* and to establish what it is we should be teaching in our classrooms. Besides creating a safe environment for learning, and promoting peace-building activities, we should teach more authentic subject matter. James Loewen's critique of the misconceptions taught in schools is a reminder that these things are still going on. James Banks, in his book *Cultural Diversity and Education* (2001) delineates what has been going on in classrooms. In terms of multicultural education, his main focus of interest is on how much multicultural awareness is really going on. For example, he describes a teaching approach embraced by most teachers, the *contributions* and *additive approaches*. By these, he means that teachers incorporate the *contributions* of a cultural group, per haps once a year, conveniently, let's say, during the Thanksgiving holidays. So, students learn about Native Americans and their contributions to North American society. That's it, book closed, we've done multiculturalism for the year. This is usually the norm, in many schools today.

Or, perhaps, teachers become more ambitious and they try to add or include a few more interesting tidbits about people of color (this would be the *additive approach*). Hence, perhaps during Black History Month, St. Patrick's Day, or *Cinco de Mayo* they would include or add thoughts about African Americans, Irish people and Mexican people, in that same order. By adding on or including the study of these people and their celebrations, some teachers feel that they have accomplished the mandates of multicultural education and have in some way *acculturated* their students into the ways of the world. Studying the lifestyles and contributions of people is not enough. Banks exhorts teachers and administrators in schools to truly embrace the goals of multicultural education and to change the curriculum so that there is a real exposure to the goals of multicultural education.

In so doing, Banks calls for a total re-haul of the educational program. His recommendation is to embrace a *transformation approach* where everybody becomes an agent of change. Through this transformation of the curriculum, school environment, and treatment of multicultural issues, an informed, global perspective would most likely appear. Banks is very interested in a global citizenship concept. He believes that we must educate future generations to become peaceful participants of a global world that contributes to the welfare of the world. We cannot continue isolating ourselves from the rest of the world and instead, should incorporate ways of embracing global diversity actively.

As a classroom teacher, I always used such opportunities as the Columbus and Thanksgiving stories to branch out and learn more about the *age of exploration*, about the navigational tools and obstacles that existed during the Middle Ages and into the Renaissance. I use a timeline in class to provide my students with a context they can relate to. We work on maps, look at scientific discoveries that were made back then, and read some of the literature written in earlier times. We often find time to act out certain events and to really live them, instead of reading stories about them.

Another teaching suggestion I make is to promote a three-pronged approach to learning. Instead of siding with the heroes and heroines of the story, I ask my college students to explore the roles of all participants. Hence, as college students prepare lesson plans for their own future students, I ask them to *multiculturalize* their units and to think in a three-pronged manner. Hence, the role of the protagonists, antagonists, and victorious characters become important and are read in a new light. So, when studying the history of the American Revolutionary War, I expect students to give me personalized accounts of what the British, the French and the Native American troops were doing during these events.

THEORIES ON HUMAN ISSUES

As we begin to define who it is that we really are, let's explore what have been perennial and important questions shared by humanity as a whole. So, when the *race* issue pops up, what do you think? Is race a biological feature? Is there such a thing as race or ethnicity? Personally, I have problems with this as I fill out application forms. I leave this portion of the application form blank because there's no slot for my race, which is human race. I don't think we can slot people into racial categories and I strongly feel that we all belong to the human race.

Another interesting topic is that of our *ethnicity*. This, I agree, clearly defines us and houses us within a particular group. So, for the purposes of this textbook, we define ethnicity as a group of people with a common culture.

I would like to pick up on the idea of racism, because although we've agreed that there are no racial differences among human beings, they in turn are overtly racist with each other. I have hence come to understand, that schools and other places where human interaction evolves constantly harbors what in the field is called *institutionalized racism*.

Institutionalized Racism is represented as forms of social discrimination and other institutionally sanctioned or even legalized practices designed to keep the dominant group in power. This means that we accept discriminatory actions allowing unequal or unfair treatment of individuals and racist practices to happen right beneath our noses without doing something to stop them.

With respect to schools, a form of *institutionalized racism* is the way we tend to lump all underrepresented youth into one slot and either send all nonnative language-speakers to ESL resource services or *track* our African American or low Socioeconomic level students into learning groups with lower-achieving learning formats. The *self-fulfilling prophecy* of doom and failure almost tears away at these youngsters' futures as we decide whether they will make it in our world.

In my college lecture hall, as I describe these situations, I urge my students to stop for a moment and to make a conscientious decision to stop these negative actions on youngsters. I ask my students the following:

1. To become more informed about the ways these youngsters are dealt with,
2. To develop research-informed mechanisms whereby they can integrate these students better and to make them feel they are a part of the classrooms they will be teaching in.
3. To learn to diversify instruction so that all youngsters in any classroom are taught in the specific learning-style preference they learn best in.

This leads me to include a large piece, which involves our understanding of ourselves as cultural beings. As we progress in our personal exploration and define our cultural inclinations, it is also important to explore the cultural identities of our future students. In so doing, I urge teacher-candidates to try to link home, neighborhood, and community into their instruction. As culturally aware teachers, we need to start getting to know our students outside the school walls. As we get to know them better, we will most probably be able to reach them better.

THEORIES ON CROSS CULTURAL TEACHING

Through my personal research interests, I have *triangulated* some useful information about two distinct student populations (Hispanic/Latino and Native American.) As we uncover and discover how they learn best and how to teach them more effectively, we will probably resolve one of the most salient issues in our teaching career, that of integrating our students into our classrooms.

Let's begin with the Hispanic/Latino Learners. This is a community of learners that I know well, as I too define myself as a Latina. I won't get into a discussion here of what's the most politically correct nomenclature, Hispanic or Latino. To me, they are the same. However, Hispanic incorporates European Spanish-speaking individuals and Latino focuses more on North, Central, and South American. The Spanish-speaking individuals of the Americas also identify themselves with their aboriginal, native heritage and feel that the term Hispanic excludes these. I won't get into colonial and post-colonial perspectives either, because this discussion will throw me off into a focus that is not necessary for this forum.

As I read more and more about ways to teach Latino/Hispanic students better, and I reflect on my own past experiences as a classroom teacher, let me explain what research indicates as best practices and what I would agree with. Let's explore the concept of *field-dependence*, which instructionally means that a student needs lots of one-on-one, personalized, contractual and contact-laden assistance in order to learn a skill. An example of this in the classroom is when students require lots of modeling and direct feedback from their teacher.

As I look back into my own world, growing up in Latin America, I recall family and classroom interactions where the expectation of *field-dependence* was embedded in our lifestyle. A field-dependent individual will always seek confirmation and reaffirmation from an adult who is working with him/her. In a way, it's a form of parenting that most Hispanic/Latino children are used to and expect as they interact with their teachers. A concrete example, let's say, would be a young child learning to fasten her shoelaces. She will break the task up into small steps and probably seek eye contact or encouraging words from a parent or caregiver. This type of coaxing encouragement is almost a means of communication and a very Latino way of projecting affection towards the little one. In the classroom, teachers embody this parental figure as they deliver instruction, often pausing to have students repeat what the teacher has just said, or expecting students to finish her sentence as an instructional format. This recitative way of teaching is handed down from generation to generation and I would say, becomes a way of life. In conversations with colleagues from other Spanish speaking North-American countries I find that this teacher-parent relationship also exists elsewhere. To illustrate, a Puerto Rican colleague explained to a group of North American teachers in Western New York the following vignette. No matter what happens in the classroom, as soon as instruction concludes, the teacher begins to sing a song, students sing along with her and this becomes, like our bell-system, the transition from subject to subject or class to class. Whatever negative or non-productive activity went on prior to this sing-along is forgotten and everything is forgiven.

Looking more closely at a typical Latino/Hispanic classroom, I would say that it is teacher-directed and that most instruction is initiated and controlled by the teacher. Hence, if you expect students who hail from these countries to initiate activity or to participate avidly in group-related work, don't count on it happening, because they're not used to it. It's better to allow them to watch others and to let them phase-in to your classroom environment slowly. I would also recommend that while carrying out group-work let them sit with a more capable-peer for a while so they can watch how others work. Again, watching more capable peers at work is also a very Latino practice, almost part of our life-style. Lots of learning occurs through observation, allow your Latino newcomer to watch and imitate other classmates. Another important thing to remember is that, again, because of our parenting/teaching styles, youngsters in Hispanic/Latino classrooms will come up to the teacher frequently seeking eye-contact, a pat on the back and immediate approval and reassurance. Don't be surprised if your students seek you out often. They won't go back to their seats unless you've given the kinds of loving assurance, eye contact and an indication that everything is o.k.

As we continue to explore research-based, cultural learning information about Latino students further, we discover that:

1. They are group-oriented. Don't expect lots of individualized work from them and foster more group-work activities.
2. They are *inductive thinkers*. We need to prod deeply to elicit responses from them. This comes from parenting and family settings where youngsters seldom initiate interactions with adults.
3. They are *peer-oriented*, seeking group approval for their actions.
4. They have an *external locus of control*, which means that they frequently seek verbal rewards.

In terms of authority figures, when you confront them, they will usually react to you with fear. It's very hard to strike up a conversation in class where you'd ask them for feedback on what they did or are doing. However, if you wish to communicate effectively, personal and informal situations work better.

The next cultural group that we will explore is the Native American learner. I do not belong to this group, yet hold them close to my heart. From conversations with many Seneca Nation, Abenake, and Métis friends that I have cultivated in my life, I couldn't agree more with the following learning preferences. From what I know about these various Native American people, their lives are built around their community. Sharing of resources and cooperative learning are key formats in which families and their communities interact. Another feature that I've learned about most Native American people I've encountered is their management of silence. I observed how paused and almost solemnly they pace their utterances so as not to disturb the natural order of things. I have seldom interacted with a loud, vociferous Native American child. The other culturally based piece of wisdom that I have accumulated is the way they handle time. From conversations with friends, I've learned that time is negotiated constantly. Sometimes it's the right time for doing things and sometimes not. It's almost a visceral form of knowing. Individuals have a sense that perhaps it's better to wait than to act abruptly. So, in your classrooms, if you encounter quiet, passive, and very calm students, let them be the way they are and let them manifest themselves to you on their own, don't prod or nag them.

Native American students do communicate and do participate in classroom instruction. They do, however, have a code of understanding whereby they wait to see who should really go first in group-interaction. They are used to this from relating to the elders and more-capable peers in their communities, where an honor system exists. You are entitled to speak when you know what you are going to say, and you remain quiet if you have nothing to contribute.

This very simple, yet knowledge-laden way of being needs to be respected and upheld in today's classrooms.

Actually, I think we learn a lot from this and I would most probably invite members of this community to talk to my students and to enlighten us about ways of being with each other. In terms of classroom activity and interaction, teachers should ensure that their classroom rules and classroom environment acknowledges the advantages of this type of respect for one another.

Theories on Culturally-informed Instruction

This brief exploration leads us to what we really have to do and know about as we develop instructional materials to teach these youngsters. Some classroom applications that are important to consider are:

1. Co-educational issues
2. Turn taking
3. Attention-seeking-behaviors
4. Value systems

How do we manage these in our classrooms? What are some choices we need to consider? As we group our students into pairs, triads, or groups of four, do we diversify? What works best? My advice to you is to group students according to the task at hand and to ensure that the group is well balanced. Keep the coeducational group-issues in mind for other things, but not for group functionality.

In terms of turn taking, don't allow the more dominant peers to oppress the less verbal students. Create classroom rules that empower all your students to speak up and speak out. Attention-seeking behaviors should be discouraged. Students who act-up in class are your typical *classroom delayers* who want you to slow down so that they can continue carrying out their prankish behavior. Don't allow this and don't reinforce it. If a student needs to consult with you, encourage him/her to consult with other team-members first, and then to seek you out when their other options have already been explored. You'll be surprised at finding out how we can stretch our frustration threshold and build tolerance for ambiguity.

PRACTICE EXERCISE

Before you reflect on your own value system, on the ways you react to different situations, and on the things that were handed down to you, let me share a classroom exercise that I do with my teacher education candidates. Given a simple questionnaire they are asked to consider what their tolerance threshold is. Their usual answers are "Oh, I accept everybody. I'm tolerant of people's differences. I'm not a racist. I don't intimidate others." I ask them to jot down these first comments as we discuss classroom issues in greater depth.

We later focus on what it is that makes us react in certain ways to such things as dress, style, and other grooming preferences. Pretty soon, some unexpected reactions spring up. These are usually mild in the sense that, teacher candidates express simple likes and dislikes. For example, they share concerns over people wearing certain types of clothing, essences, and sports-related garments. They also share their concerns over people's personal habits (smoking, personal grooming, attire). Here's where we begin to uncover the layers we all have within our tolerance threshold. We now concur that we all have these unexplored and very subtle levels of intolerance.

We then move on to people's belief systems. Here is where students begin to side with one another, especially when they explore religious views. As they begin to talk to one another about their inherited and acquired religions, they then speak about their national origins and how these shape their lives. The core layer begins to appear. Teacher candidates begin mentioning the ways in which family members express themselves about their family origins and affiliations. We ask, are we tolerant of the Italian relative, of the newly immigrated Irish relative, of the non-Jewish sister in law?

"I'm not prejudiced! I treat them nicely and always make a point of being polite!"

"But, sometimes I hear racial slurs within the family, one cousin nudging another saying

"Did you see the way in which she..."

As we begin to explore this core, we are more ready to receive the kind of information that a multicultural education course tends to deliver.

Based on these ideas, use the table below to reflect on what you identify with, how you deal with these culturally based ideas and how you define yourself as an individual. For example, think of the way you act and react when in a large crowd. Who do you gravitate to and why? How do you define yourself? Who taught you this? Explore your core value system and then move on to your opinions and thoughts about cultural groups. This is a personal reflection that need not be shared, so take your time to candidly respond to as many issues and questions that you might have.

How I define myself:
Culturally: I come from

_____

_____

_____

I have learned cultural behavior from

_____

_____

_____

I have had _____exposure to cultural differences
_____a little _____ a lot _____ none at all

When I walk into a room where I stand out for being different, I feel:

_____

_____

_____

I have been in situations where other people have experienced this and I have:

_____

_____

_____

REFLECTION EXERCISES

(1) Now that you've carried out this exercise, give yourself some time to re-flect. How do you feel about your value system? What things do you need to adjust or change? Did you find anything unexpected about yourself?

_____

_____

_____

_____

(2) Film-Review
Give yourself time now to explore all of the above as you do the film-review exercise. I'd like you to choose from any film you have seen recently in the past involving teachers in schools, classroom-based activity or contemporary educational issues. You might want to do this with a partner. View the film one more time and jot down the layers of culture that you observe as well as the layers of human interaction. As you do this, jot down the kinds of things we have discussed in this chapter. Enjoy this exercise

_____

_____

_____

_____

_____

Chapter Two

Identity-formation

This chapter deals with *identity-formation*. In it we explore our cultural identities and those of our students. As we start exploring how a deep understanding of self leads to a strong identity-building foundation, we begin to embrace the *equity principle* and to teach all students so that in fact no child is left behind. We explore our own biases and impediments that could have sent strong negative messages to our peers and students. In doing so, we talk about the *Deficit Model/Deficit Orientation* (Banks, 2003.) We also explore the term *ethnocentrism* and how it affects our teaching. We then start to explore the history of how multicultural education was excluded from the curriculum.

Based on the ideas of equitable educational opportunities for all learners, we focus on *student-centered instruction*. This leads us to move from focusing on teaching and the teacher to focusing on the pupil/student and learner. We analyze teaching and learning styles to better understand the filters and channels necessary for providing instruction in a safe classroom environment. In so doing, we also explore the concept of a safe, equitable, empathetic, and nurturing classroom environment. Re-reading a classic book and responding to it with our newly found *multicultural lens* is an activity that accompanies this chapter.

THEORIES ON INTEGRATING MULTICULTURAL EDUCATION

I am frequently asked: Why do we need multicultural education?

Here are some justifications from the literature in the field: "In urban areas minority and low-income students are most likely to be taught by teachers who are "inadequately prepared, inexperienced, and ill-qualified"

15

(Darling-Hammond, 1995). If the academic outcomes for minority and low-income children are to change, aggressive action must be taken to change the caliber and quantity of learning opportunities they encounter." (James Banks, 2004). Lastly, in order to meet the multiple requirements necessary to earn accreditation:

NCATE:
1. Recognizes the political, social, and economic realities that individuals experience in culturally diverse and complex human encounters.
2. Reflects the importance of culture, race, sexuality and gender, ethnicity, religion, socioeconomic status, and exceptionalities in the educational process.

At this point, to ease into a discussion on the reasons for teaching multicultural education, I'd like to explain what I think happens when we deal with cultural differences. Either from past experiences, or as a result of what we were taught in school or at home, or because of lack of information, human beings do not relate well with differences. As you saw earlier, children react to differences and manifest these quite openly. Historically as well, we have been taught that some cultures have conquered others. Some of the stories we were taught in history class (Loewen, 2001) present some cultures and some nations as superior to others. Hence, in our *collective conscience*, we have been taught about a deficit orientation. I'd like to address this concept before engaging you in some thought about humanity and its evolution.

A *deficit orientation*, in lay terms is an oppressive form of thinking where the stronger or more powerful entity views others as inferior. Authors in this field have represented this view in many ways. I want to focus on how we deal with this issue in schools and with children and parents of the communities that we teach. Having taught in international schools for over twenty years, I have been exposed to people of different national origins, ethnicities, and belief systems. I have taught children from many nations, religious views, and family traditions. I too am a person of multiple ethnicities and have experienced the deficit model first-hand. It's a subtle form of rejection whereby one individual makes the other feel inferior, unwelcome, incompetent, or merely an outsider. In schools, I've seen this as it is applied to transfer students. Staff, administrators, or teachers make the child and parents feel like the child will never catch up because he/she has missed so much school. This reality can be seen on the playground where the newest member of the group finds himself isolated and alienated by peers. Ultimately, this situation dooms the child into a *self-fulfilling prophecy* of failure. I've just provided a very simple example to help explain what I think is done to students and their families as they enter our schools for the first time.

This situation extends and spreads in many different ways. Underrepresented youth in many North American schools are treated this way all the time. Their records aren't explored properly and they are usually lumped together in special education groups not allowing them to benefit from the educational services they are entitled to receive.

A *deficit orientation* is also present in the way we communicate with each other. We are so used to fighting over who has power and control that we have stopped communicating properly. We either yell louder than others, or use all other types of attention-seeking devices to retain and maintain this power and control.

An example of this *deficit orientation* in communication is when a teacher addresses her students expecting their full cooperation, this being a message to *shut up and listen* without inviting the students to challenge her position or to participate in the conversation. I'm sure you can come up with many examples of the deficit model in action. And, I'd like you to do so during the reflective part of this chapter. Think of the many ways you were put down by somebody? Perhaps you did it to others? I'd like you to think about this as we read about how people from different cultures and different ways of knowing deal with everyday things, communicate and work. In this way, as you become acclimatized and acculturated to the different ways of knowing and doing things by other people, you will develop a broader understanding of these differences. Ultimately, your knowledge and enlightened information will ensure that the deficit orientation does not permeate your classrooms and halls.

THEORIES ON EARLY HUMAN THOUGHT

As we explore cultural diversity issues, it is always good to trace everything back to our origins as human beings. In order to do so, I'm going to walk you through the ways people thought and did things as they evolved into the 21st century. Let's begin with what in the literature is referred to as pre-literate people. You have probably referred to early man as the caveman. Let's revisit this era by picturing a day in the life of a man, woman, of children and perhaps of an entire community as they lived day by day. As hunters and gatherers what mattered most for these people was their survival. Their basic needs had to be met daily. To ensure this they needed to develop a keen sense of observation, to design effective tools and efficient survival strategies. Without going into much detail, and reinforced by the many stories we were told as children including perhaps a few cave-drawings, we learn that man was a communal, social being, who depended on his community for survival.

I think this is an important fact to remember as we plan for authentic and lasting forms of instruction for our learners.

Man continues to be a communal, social being who depends on others to move on in life. Take a close look at yourself as a student or teacher. Don't you enjoy talking about what you do best with others? Don't you seek others to share your progress or to seek advice? Watch the children you work with. They play with each other and watch each other perform different tasks. This is all part of that communal being, and in a Vygotskian framework (1958), a socially constructed way of being and doing. Keep this in mind always as you plan instructional opportunities for yourself and your students. Learning is a socially constructed activity.

We've overdone and overused the industrialized educational model. The cookie-cutter format used in the nineteenth century was designed so that each individual would learn to be productive in the newly industrialized society. That was back then, when obedient, rule-abiding citizens were needed to form a society based on mass-production and mass-consumption of items.

We have now evolved into another era where there's a new mindset brewing. Individualization, a quest for knowledge, and a competitive world, where skills and know-how are no longer a ticket to life-long employment are the survival tactics. Globalization, *outsourcing*, manufacturing *layoffs* and *Fortune 500* company closures are the facts of the twenty-first century. If we can't do the job, somebody else, anywhere in the world will be able to do it for much less money. With modernized travel and communication systems, companies in the United States can have their paperwork processed somewhere in Ireland, overnight, and delivered by courier the next day. You've all received telemarketing calls from people in India trying to sell you a technological device or to align with a new communications system. This is the savvy of this century, the global world where we need to learn a new language of effective, work-based, international skills. We no longer master the skills of one trade, but on the contrary, become informed of future skills that we'll have to master if we want to remain on the job market.

In terms of teaching and learning, the dynamics of a schoolroom have also changed. While we teach our students, they learn much more of what they want to know on their own. They access whatever game or web-site and develop fingertip skills that we never had. I'm sure that many of your students can access information that you're not even aware of. In many cases, students are more knowledgeable about certain things than their teachers! So, classrooms have a different tone to them, and teachers need to realize this.

During the industrial era and unfortunately, for a long period later, students were passive recipients of a teacher's autocratic instruction. Rote learning and many forms of this cookie-cutter format I've talked about abounded in classrooms. Actually, the skills-driven format is still used in many classrooms today. You will still see teacher-driven instruction and youngsters sitting in straight rows listening to the teacher and filling out copious worksheets. I cringe, when I visit a classroom where the teacher has just finished inspiring students with a story and doles out a skills-laden worksheet that has nothing to do with the story but reinforces some grammatical skill they need to master. I squirm when I look at reading and writing programs that use storytelling and good literature for the wrong reasons, like, O.k. let's read Charlotte's Web to learn how to punctuate dialogue in a sentence. No, let's read this fabulous story by E.B. White to learn about farm animals and farm life, or to learn about how spiders spun their webs, or to learn about language! Ultimately, let's read this story to cultivate a lifelong enjoyment of reading! I shouldn't be destroying a system that is in place in many schools today.

There is a form of scripted reading and writing that is much needed to offer a foundational literacy knowledge base to underrepresented youth. Schools where English is not the prevailing language, need to offer their students a sound and solid language-base as a common denominator towards literacy development. However, teachers should use these instructional formats as opportunities to cultivate a broader knowledge base and to imbue their students with a desire to know more about topics and trends. So, I encourage you to explore more contemporary teaching options that include skills building and a quest for deeper knowledge.

In the context of multicultural education, as we begin to understand how different communities engage in communication and learning, we attest to the fact that many cultures have kept this primeval mode of engaging in learning as a social activity. It comes from our roots as human beings striving to survive. Hence, let's explore the ways people think about things and the ways communal life-styles continue to permeate out cultural existence.

THEORIES ON EARLY FOLKTHOUGHT

Again, in an effort to understand where many of the things that we think, do, and say come from, we will explore early ways of thinking, which we will call *folkthought* (Bogardus, 1940). It is amazing to find that the ways our ancestors processed their belief systems and accounted for the realities pervades in our thinking today.

To begin our discussion, *folkthought* permeated primitive religions. Preliterate societies believed their fate was governed by spirits or gods and hence moderated their behavior around these. Their actions regulated their ideas, and they were most concerned with ways in which they pleased or offended these spirits.

If we look at distinct communities and their folkthought, we might find the key to understanding why these cultural and national groups think the way they do. For example, early African communities thought that evil would haunt evildoers. They cultivated a strong sense of leadership where groups sought refuge in their leader's decisions and choices.

People of the Orient upheld filial relationships, honoring their ancestry and thus harboring respect for elders. They believed that scholarship and learning influenced the group over individuals and that kindness was the greatest personality trait.

In European folkthought the role of friendship was important. There was also an awareness of group psychology.

Early American Indian and Mexican folkthought was of a practical nature, dealing with personality development and a sense of organization. American Indian proverbs reveal careful observation and shrewd generalizations. Experience is valued as a great teacher.

I invite you to corroborate all of the above by exploring folk-tales and legends handed down from generation to generation. Your classroom libraries should be richly laden with books about people everywhere. Create a story-time section where you share legends about people from all over the world and begin to compare their distinctive folkthought. Make yours a cross-cultural classroom where second-graders can explore these sophisticated ideas with you and with each other. Raise inter-cultural awareness early on, beginning with your early childhood program. We need to acquaint our learners with the ways that people do things and think about things differently and similarly, so that we can enhance the tolerance threshold we so much strive for.

RAISING INTER-CULTURAL & CROSS-CULTURAL CONSCIOUSNESS USING LITERATURE

After having read about the different ways people from different ethnicities interpret the world, it's nice to look back at our own learning experiences and to draw from what we have learned about the world as children.

For this exercise, I have my college students explore literature from their elementary and middle school years. This helps develop a deeper sense of inter-cultural and cross-cultural awareness that leads to a keener sense of self. Hopefully, as we explore the themes brought out in the book selections we will share shortly, we will make conscious observations about social justice and will also glean meaningful experiences. Learning about bias, prejudice, and institutionalized racism is not easily done without some form of personal investment. The reason for this is that the cold facts don't have such an impact on students unless they connect fact to personal experience. Hence, thoughts, feelings and issues aren't as easily dealt with and dismissed through lecture notes and multiple choice exam questions. Dealing with issues of tolerance requires:

1. Learning how to tune into one's own lived experiences.
2. Having a non-judgmental platform in which to express one's voice.
3. Finding a narrative in which to do so.

LEARNING BY CRITIQUING JUVENILE LITERATURE

After selecting a list of books that we will enjoy reading or re-reading in the college classroom, I attempt to create a book-club-style environment where the themes and topics in the book invade those impeding silences. As college students revisit these novels, stories, and tales, they begin to explore a heightened sense of awareness that they had never experienced before.

As we explore the multiple themes throughout the semester, the most powerful one is that of the newly acquired sense of knowing which results from this personal exploration brought about from re-reading the texts from our childhood.

My own personal experience helps me bridge the silences and sudden insights providing me with a sound knowledge base on selected classroom texts. Having been a classroom teacher myself, I have read and re-read many of the chosen texts. Some of the selections we use for classroom discussions are all-time favorites like E.B. White's *Charlotte's Web*, *Stuart Little*, or *Trumpet of the Swan*, Laura Ingalls Wilder's Prairie Series and Louisa May Alcott's *Little Women*, *Little Men*, among many. Students with middle school and high school preferences conjure such titles as William Golding's *Lord of the Flies*, George Orwell's *1984*, and Mark Twain's *Tom Sawyer* and *Huckleberry Finn* among others. I recommend books like Ernest Hemingway's *The Old Man and the Sea*, or Salinger's *Catcher in the Rye*, S.E. Hinton's *The Outsiders*, John Steinbeck's *Of Mice & Men*, *Grapes of Wrath* among others. These books are very well written offering a rich insight into the lives of people from other lands inserted in the North American panorama.

We just haven't stopped to look at the ways the African Americans or Asian Pacific Islanders were treated in such narratives as Steinbeck's, which are laden with examples of discrimination towards these underrepresented groups.

During our school years, we usually read about the protagonist and his/her plight. Our classroom teachers encourage us to look at setting, characters and plot, ultimately to have us finish the book in time for the book-report due date. I have yet to recall a classroom teacher who had me understand the plight of the underrepresented, the exploited, or the discriminated-against characters in a classic such as all of the above. All of these other characters helped build the story line and diversified the characters and setting to make them more intriguing. Honestly, if I look back at what I read about and watched in movies and on television, back in the 1950's I don't think underrepresented people were highlighted or explored in depth at all! I invite you to join me in rereading or reviewing old westerns, old versions of these classics and basically anything approved by the McArthyan Hollywood era to see how the treatment of other ethnicities was carried out. You'd be surprised at what you find.

In so doing, with my own college students, we begin broaching the topic of intolerance by informally discussing issues that are commonly viewed by all of us through informal class discussions. The conversations become more agitated as students become more involved and invested in the discussion and feel that they have a common knowledge base with peers. At times, I personally experience wonderful flashbacks of my own fourth-grade classroom. I taught fourth grade for twelve years and cherish every memory. I guess this was and continues to be my favorite age group, as youngsters still like their teacher, make intergenerational and inter-gender friendships well and relate well to new learning. I could still cultivate that sense of wonder and awe with my fourth graders year-round. Let me share a slice of these memories with you.

MEMORIES FROM MY FOURTH-GRADE CLASSROOM

I taught elementary school from 1978 until 1984. I enjoyed introducing creative literacy activities in my fourth grade classroom back in the 80's, at the height of the Whole Language Movement. My nine and ten-year old students were empowered when given the task of critiquing a book or editing somebody else's draft in progress. Clipboards for correcting and director-turned-author-hairs were conjured for class discussions. These episodes brought out the movie critic in the students-turned-editors.

It was always amusing to listen to their conclusions, as they compared the movie version of *Charlotte's Web* (E.B.White) to the book. It was always a pleasure to see the outcome of such dynamic discussion:

"I prefer the book!"

"They left out the best part!"

"You miss out on the way in which the word was found and produced."

This same empowered energy leads us to explore the themes of intolerance, prejudice, scape-goating, and institutional racism with concrete examples. It also offers a common ground for exploring themes that haven't been so relevant to us in the past.

Re-reading Harper Lee's, *To Kill a Mockingbird* or John Steinbeck's *Of Mice and Men* or S.E. Hinton's *The Outsiders* students explore the way in which tolerance and cultural awareness need to be learned. When they read these novels for the first time, as adolescents in middle school, they were able to discern the injustice, rivalry, bullying, and coarse language found in the texts. They were also able to side with protagonists, to identify sources of rivalry, and to speak about surfacing issues of racism and intolerance.

Given an assignment to explore these themes more profoundly, college-level students then begin to uncover layers of knowledge they had never visited before. For example, in *To Kill a Mockingbird* they write about the injustice towards Boo, a character in the book that is learning-challenged.

They are appalled at the treatment of *Boo*, first as the prime suspect of the crime due to his disability and social position, and also because he is the perfect scapegoat; an outcast. Next, they are surprised that Boo has had no formal schooling. His disability goes untreated in the early 1900's, when there must have been other cases like his. Students bring out many characteristics in Boo that they hadn't related to when reading the text in grade seven.

Interestingly, enough, they also bring out other issues, such as sexism. The little girl in the text (Scout) is quite an independent thinker. She and her brother are equals. Her father, *Atticus,* empowers her giving her the same responsibilities he gives her brother.

Another theme that arises is that of the spirituality and strength of the house-keeper, an African American matron who assists the family. Atticus allows her to become a foster parent to his children, letting her participate in family affairs, to engage in conversation and to share family life.

Selecting children's literature like this is a helpful tool in developing the kinds of critical awareness we will require in order for us to deal with issues of social justice in the future. The plots and themes provide insights into another society and its culture. Here are some other titles with suggested exploration ideas that your own students would enjoy exploring.

1. Karen Hesse. (1997). *Out of the Dust*. NY: Scholastic.

   A *Newberry Award* winning novel, the author takes us to the North American prairies during the great draught leading to the Great Depression. The diary entries begin in 1920 when Billie Jo, the protagonist experiences life and loss in an Oklahoma wheat farm. Through her eyes, the reader relives the hopeless years that converted the prairies into an endless dustbowl.

2. Mary Lyons. (1992). *Letters from a Slave Girl, the story of Harriet Jacobs*. NY: Simon & Schuster.

Mary Lyons, after careful research, reconstructs the life of a slave girl. Harriet Jacobs reveals, in her diary letters, the many secrets she had to conceal throughout her enslaved childhood. Aside from evidence of physical and sexual abuse, the accounts are detailed revelations of escape, torture, disenfranchisement and despair during pre-Civil War America.

3. Lois Lowry. (1989). *Number the Stars*. NY: Laurel Leaf.

The story takes place in Copenhagen, Denmark in 1943. Two close childhood friends experience the Nazi invasion and deportation. Through their eyes, the reader is able to witness harsh changes, rough decisions and a total change of pace.

These are titles of contemporary issues of war and strife that I would only recommend if you have already prepared the terrain and created a knowledge-base in your students that allows them to explore these topics in full safety. During my own schooling, I guess because I grew up after *World War II*, during *The Vietnam War* as well as *The Cold War* certain topics were glossed over. I guess that the international school that I attended was afraid that we would utter the word communism and God forbid become convinced that it was good or bad. Back then, during the Cold War years, such terms were not pronounced, let alone in the classroom. Hence, I never learned about the *Cultural Revolution* in China, where families who did not abide by the Communist regime were in peril. I never learned about the fact that the Cultural Revolution set out to erase the Chinese memory, burning family heirlooms and effigies of the past. The Cultural Revolution also sought to nationalize people's mindsets, not allowing citizens to read, learn about or know anything about the world. Hence, books, musical instruments, and anything that was westernized was burned, eliminated or thrown out.

During my school days, towards eighth grade, we were finally informed about the real world through a publication called *Current Events,* which gave us an update of what was happening around the world. You too, have probably had access to a similar publication called Weekly Reader. I encourage you to explore these topics, to prepare your students with facts and realities of what they will read and to keep them informed of the cruelty that continues to exist in the world. Hence, the following three books will give them insights of contemporary warring nations and the strife of their people.

4. Elaine Mar (1999) *Paper Daughter: Story of travels from China*. Perennial/ Harper Collins, NY.

5. Elmaz Abinader (1997). *Children of the Roojme: A Family's Journey from Lebanon*. The University of Wisconsin Press.
6. Karl Bruckner (1962). *The Day of the Bomb*. Great Britain, Butler & Tanner, Ltd.

MORE INTERESTING CRITIQUING OPPORTUNITIES

This is another classroom exercise that I've enjoyed doing in Higher Education. You might cater it to your elementary or middle school classroom. So many of the classics we've re-read have been made and even re-made into movies, that it's a good classroom exercise to critique them as a group. Some titles that I've enjoyed working with are:

1. *The Outsiders*, S.E. Hinton
2. *Of Mice and Men*, John Steinbeck
3. *Charlie & the Chocolate Factory*, Roald Dahl
4. *Jane Eyre*, Emily Bronte
5. *The Scarlet Letter*, Nathaniel Hawthorne

It is amazing how students find new topics to explore and forms of racial/ethnic and social discrimination that they hadn't seen at an earlier viewing.

Some students have enjoyed adding new titles to my collection. I recall one in particular that surprised me. The series where actress *Reese Witherspoon* represents blondes, Legally Blonde and Legally Blonde II has had quite an impact on people with blonde hair. The insights gleaned from the self-fulfilling prophecy of failure as it relates to blonde people are interesting. Other students have enjoyed watching more violent movies like American History X, which I would only recommend for higher education settings, but not for elementary and middle school students. I invite you to come up with titles of your own.

We could take the entire film remake concept and do comparisons with these. Perhaps you might notice that more contemporary versions deal with these issues differently because they either have to or have become aware of the political correctness they have to abide by, and ultimately, their importance.

Take for example the remake of *Around the World in Eighty Days* (2004) based on the Jules Verne novel with the same title. I'm sure the earlier version (circa 1960's) makes politically incorrect mistakes that have had to be corrected for today's audiences.

PRACTICE EXERCISE

Using the examples that I have shared with you, try to develop your very own model of literature-based unit. Pick a few of your favorite books and assemble your package. Don't get carried away with too many details and start preparing materials for your students. Remember, it's about their ideas, not yours.

_____

_____

_____

_____

_____

REFLECTION EXERCISE

At this point, having thought out a unit of instruction, anticipated the areas you'll want your students to explore, and having done some soul-searching for yourselves, what impact has this exercise had on you? Jot down your reflections. Remember, when you write things down, these develop a life of their own.

_____

_____

_____

_____

Chapter Three

Our Cultural Capital to *Broker* our Teaching

THEORIES ON TEACHING

Chapter three focuses on teacher-empowerment. In today's world, teachers have developed a cultural capital of their own. They know about people and cultures in a very unique and informed manner. Teachers are cultural brokers as they incorporate their knowledge into what they teach and insert novel learning environments for their students to experience.

Teachers bring a lot of experience and savvy into many educational contexts. They become invested in teaching and learning in a way that is unique and exiting. You might agree with me in the following statement; teachers enjoy what they do and are usually invested in what they teach. Teachers learn lots of first hand knowledge about a lot of things through their teaching. I for one, became an expert in the many avenues of learning that I embarked on, namely so that I could teach them better. This means that when I explored the many Native American nations around the United States and Canada, I learned every detail I could learn about to teach them well. When I taught geography and history, I did extensive research on my own, becoming well aware of the existing nuances and misconceptions about the world in order to teach true facts and to promote a love for learning and for research in my students. The same is true for all of the other subjects that I taught. I embraced teaching as a quest for knowledge and ensured I passed on this torch to all of my students. Hence, I acquired cultural capital and became a cultural broker in doing so. I invite all teachers to follow this path to teaching and learning.

I will now share one of my true passions. The material that follows is a result of many years of research and study. I acquired cultural capital on a topic that I had a passion for during my adolescence and brokered into my elementary school and college teaching. This material has been presented to the public in different formats (university course, conference presentations, and scholarly publications).

Teachers usually have a passion of some kind. I for one, collect personal narratives by child protagonists. I've been doing this ever since I first read The Diary of Anne Frank as an adolescent. I've been finding similar titles and putting them on my book-case. Eventually, my collection became a course; (Transcultural Literature, summer, 2002) conference presentations; (TESOL 2002), in-service teacher-workshops; (Western New York 2002/2003), and finally, an article published in a journal.

I think teachers are cultural brokers and change agents. I invite you to go home right now and look through the things that matter to you. Take something from these collections and present them to your students with enthusiasm. Infuse your classes with what you do so well. You'll see a total transformation in the life of our classroom and your teaching environment.

An article that I recently published, *Child-Protagonists: The Anne Frank's of Today* Multicultural Education (Volume 11, Number 2, Winter 2003, Caddo Gap Press) reflects my feelings about first-person narratives written by children. I have been writing this article all of my life. It is a collection of the stories that I enjoyed reading from puberty until now. It begins with my favorite book, *The Diary of Ann Frank*. I was drawn to this book, not only because Anne's life mirrored my own, but also because of the coming of age issues she shared within it. I realized at that early age (12) that I enjoyed sharing a personal perspective.

My teacher-candidates also share this affinity to personal narratives and we talk about the many books that have been published after Anne Frank's Diary. These real scenarios are helpful in teaching about the world, about different customs and traditions, and about global realities. My graduate students also report that this genre brings their own students together as they share and discuss the growing pains experienced by the child protagonists as with the book *Letters from Rifka* by Karen Hesse (1992). Through this book, teachers can broach topics of health, cleanliness, and disease. As they discuss Rifka's life in the unsanitary, war-torn towns of Poland, they understand realities that would not have otherwise surfaced. On a more local note, stories like Rifka's entry into the United States after being quarantined on *Ellis Island* provide a first-person account of how treacherous the boat ride was, and how difficult it was not to be able to speak English. Another interesting result of reading this collection is that many of the protagonists are voracious readers and writers. Rifka, for one, read Pushkin to remember her long-lost family.

Reading *The Diary of Anne Frank* when I was twelve helped me cope with many things I couldn't talk about. Having heard first-person accounts of the Holocaust from my own parents and relatives, I was very afraid that this would happen again. I also remember feeling guilty many times, because my life was so good compared to that of my parents'. I remember being very saddened by some of the details I would hear at home, and knew that these details would surface in the book. However, I consciously glossed over the scenes of horror and concentrated on things that interested me at the time. I focused on Anne herself, as a girl my age, going through the same growing pains, interpreting the many situations her family was experiencing and, fearing what the future had in store for her.

I have grouped these diaries and letters from young girls in Europe. To reinforce some of the concepts I have talked about, I would begin by situating the reader.

Through the authentic artifacts, maps and historical accounts, I would present the political and historical situation in a manner that young adults can handle.

EUROPEAN CHILDREN'S DIARIES: THE STORIES OF ANNE, RIFKA AND ZLATA

I try to find a common theme using these books. In all three, the children keep a diary and enjoy literacy activities in a very special way. For example, Anne's diary is called "Kitty". The diary becomes Anne's soul mate and friend as well as a repository for her thoughts and fears.

In Karen Hesse's *Letters from Rifka*. Rifka contracts ringworm and loses her hair. She is then quarantined on *Ellis Island*. In New York. Her poor health produces temporary baldness, which makes her a "burden" to the state. In her plight, she continues to read Pushkin, learns to speak French and English, and teaches a Russian boy to read.

In Zlata Filipovic's Zlata's Diary. Zlata writes in a diary which she calls "Mimmy". Zlata gives us a first-person account of the war in what used to be Yugoslavia. Her diary pages are filled with familiar names (*MTV, Pepsi, Claudia Schiffer, Linda Evangelista*). It is unbelievable that a girl her age in today's day and age is experiencing similar life-struggles as

YOUNG CHILDREN'S REALITIES IN THE FAR EAST

Ji Li Jiang's *Red Scarf Girl: A memoir of the Cultural Revolution* describes a reality that I was never aware of as China, Korea, and Japan remain a mystery. Ji Li, a young protagonist describes her life, her struggles and her new reality in Communist China during the late 1960's when Mao Ze-Dong's

Communist Party Red Guard invaded homes, town, and villages seeking to eliminate family heir-looms, traditions, and the memory of a nation.

Meinert Dejong's *The House of Sixty Fathers* is the account of escape of a Chinese family from Japanese occupied territory. Tien-Pao is a ten-year old who gets left behind as he tries to conceal his pet piglet. He describes the atrocities he witnesses and the fear he experiences as he hides.

Eleanor Coerr's *Sadako and the Thousand Paper Cranes* recounts the life of Sadako, an aspiring Olympian runner, is struck with leukemia and bed-ridden. She had been exposed to radiation after the bombing of Hiroshima. This true story takes us through a saga where a child clings to life by the many paper cranes woven by children all over the world in hopes that they could keep her alive.

I encourage you to begin collecting stories like these where you can relate a child's point of view with your students to help promote a more global mindset and to perhaps broach topics that have been left out of our curricula. I also encourage you to work carefully with this concept as you lay the groundwork for reflection and peer-interaction. I would always begin a theme like this one couching it in a safe, loving environment so that your students approach some of these concepts and topics without fear.

PRACTICE EXERCISE

Now that you have experienced some of these literacy-based activities, try to design your very own personal narrative forum. As you develop this exercise, remember that you, the teacher, are a change agent, a cultural broker and that you are sharing your cultural capital. Before you begin, what is your cultural capital and what are you going to broker?

_____
_____
_____
_____

As cultural broker and change agent, what kinds of things are you going to transmit to others? What kinds of ideas are you going to share with your students?

_____
_____
_____
_____

Now that you have thought about your cultural capital and dialogued with others about your position as change agent and cultural broker, what are some things that you would plan to do with your students to share these ideas?

REFLECTION EXERCISE

An important part of planning and teaching is reflecting. We might take this opportunity to improve on what we planned and designed, or we might anticipate problems. This is why the dialogue you had previously is important. You might want to jot down some of the problems and insights you had after having done the previous exercise.

Chapter Four

Teacher as Change-agent, Negotiator & Peace-builder

Chapter four focuses on teacher as *negotiator, change-agent, and peace-builder*. *Classroom management* and instructional ideas and suggestions are presented in detail. Pre-service teachers at this point are ready to enter the field. As they begin to do so, they are given opportunities to observe what goes on in a real classroom. They are also encouraged to keep a reflective journal to document classroom realities and to plan for their classrooms of the future. The *learning center* as an instructional tool is explored.

THEORIES ON INTEGRATING MULTICULTURAL CONCEPTS

How do we integrate multicultural concepts and principles into the social studies curriculum in schools? How do we integrate and relate social studies with other disciplines?

This chapter will explore three instructional ideas:

1. Well-structured learning centers
2. Theme-based instruction
3. A classroom time-line

These instructional ideas have been tried and tested both in the college class-room and the schoolroom. Results from these innovative instructional ideas have motivated teacher-candidates and in-service teachers of social studies in elementary, middle and high schools.

In theory, multicultural education expects teachers and students to engage in meaningful learning that is socially constructed (Banks, 2001). In practice, classroom learning should empower students to do their own research and to report findings in open forums. Ideally both of these statements should inform in-service teachers and teacher-candidates to continue raising the bar and expectations for pupils as they continually attempt to implement a multicultural curriculum. Can this be done? Here are some innovative ideas that work.

For example, given an intriguing topic of choice, and in a well-managed classroom, a student should be trusted to carry out action research (interviewing people in the community, carrying out opinion surveys, and triangulating findings). Like a news reporter, a student could be encouraged to investigate a topic, put together a story, and showcase it in front of peers and colleagues. With proper guidelines and clear instructions as well as an organized menu of document-based-questions, (an approach readily utilized in middle and high schools) students can find articles in libraries, examine real artifacts, and become more involved in their own communities. Hence the kind of transformation purported by James A. Banks (2001) occurs, as students become socially involved in their topics of exploration (Sleeter & Grant, 1994).

How can we promote this type of transformation and social action in today's middle schools and high schools? The Internet and the availability of primary resources (inter-library loan, online resources, and periodicals) allow students to access real data and artifacts. Textbooks become obsolete as well-designed questions and clear data-gathering instructions replace them. The key issue lies on how we manage instruction so that we continue to provide students with the needed support and guidance to carry out their own quest for information.

A WELL-STRUCTURED LEARNING CENTER

This is an instructional idea that has proven to address this need to relate ideas and engage students in meaningful learning in the classroom. This center provides individual freedom to explore, tools, resources and supplies, and mobility needed for students to take charge of their learning. Learning centers of this kind can either be teacher or student-designed environments that include information, resources, and materials for students to engage in individual or small-group learning. To illustrate, a center could be set up using a cardboard display board propped on a desk. On one of the display board flaps, instructions might be posted. On another flap, an interactive task might be promoted. On a third flap a display of products might be generated. In this way students who work at the center have clear guidelines and a task to complete. Around the learning center area, teachers might provide students with magazine cutouts, paper, pencil, glue, scissors, and other utensils for them to process the information required.

Multiple learning centers also operate well in classrooms. These are other avenues that teachers could use to promote this type of learning. Multiple learning centers allow students to move from one station to another to complete a menu of tasks. Using this multiple center idea, teachers may either expect inter-related learning guiding students through a set of steps that must be completed prior to reaching the last center. Multiple learning centers can also focus on different centers and work independently of each other. For example, as the classroom teacher has students explore the theme of exploration and navigation, each center could illustrate one aspect of the theme. Hence, centered-learning in this format allows students to build knowledge and to interact with each other freeing the teacher to focus on individualization or for conferencing with individual students.

A THEME-BASED APPROACH

This is another instructional format that works well along the lines of primary source material and evidence-based instruction is the theme-based approach. To illustrate, in my college teaching practice, I encourage the development of integrated thematic units. These involve finding an over-arching theme or *big idea* to encapsulate all the related learning that ensues.

For example, I begin with a child's picture book called *Mr. Archimedes' Bath* by Pamela Allen (1980). The title gives it away as a pertinent historical book retelling the way in which *Archimedes* uncovered the principle of water displacement. The story recounts how each time Archimedes entered his bathtub, the water overflowed and how through different trials and tests, he hypothesized that any object placed in the water displaces it, causing the water to spill.

The beauty of his scientific method is not overlooked in the unit of study that I begin to develop as an example for my teacher-candidates. However, as I read the story, I ask students to find the social studies connection. Seeking for the over-arching theme or big idea, I encourage my teacher-candidates to relate this historic event to progress in transportation. Some students choose the topic of transportation, others choose the topic of inventions and still others take the theme of exploration as their theme of choice. To relate these topics to a historical context, and to continue inspiring my teacher-candidates, I begin to elicit historical questions. I encourage commentary on what life was like in the times of Archimedes (Ancient Greece).

A YEAR-ROUND CLASSROOM TIME-LINE

This immediately brings to the surface the need for some kind of *mnemonic device* to capture pupil interest and conjure the idea of a *classroom-sized timeline.* Here is where I suggest the use of a year-round classroom time-line. To justify this, I relate to students how important it is for young learners to understand that evolution and change occurred through long periods of time. I also emphasize the importance of understanding how through time ideas, events and environmental changes affected the way mankind evolved. I use this concept along with the time-line and them-based module to highlight the interdisciplinary potential of such an integrated topic. Finally, I try to inspire teacher-candidates to share these experiences in their host classrooms and to experiment with the idea of relating to their pupils the fact that they can take different ramifications (science and mathematics) aside from the historical one to teach more connectedly.

PUTTING ALL THREE TOGETHER
(CENTER, UNIT & TIMELINE)

Focusing on the big idea for our *theme-based unit*, and using the time-line as our resource, let's pick the themes of exploration and discovery. As I continue to read the story about Archimedes' experiments in the bathtub, I share his great discovery, reading the part where he yells out *EUREKA!* which celebrates the fact that he solved the water-displacement problem. I hold on to that wonderful word to share the importance of discovery and the gratifying feeling of closure that the possible solution or solutions bring.

This feeling of success leads me to tie in other such opportunities in history where eureka moments like this one brought humanity out of the Dark Ages and onto the Renaissance and to the *Age of Exploration.* To illustrate, I ask my students to relate this discovery to the progress made in the shipping industry after the times of Archimedes' day and to relate this with other inventions that improved travel and instrumentation. Our classroom discussions evolve around the inspiring nature of this competitive era when map-making, exploration propositions abounded and travelers challenged worldviews, bringing them to other shores.

Topics of exploration inspired by these big ideas send students on their quest to find out more about ships, ship-building improvements, compasses, other navigating devices, astronomy and its influences on navigation, and a plethora of exciting themes. Students are also asked to revisit the classroom timeline to fill in the timeframes in which each discovery was made. All of these activities (learning center, theme-based lessons and continuous time-line) almost have a built-in-clause requiring students to access primary sources and to respond to document-based or evidence-based instruction. In a nutshell, all of the above formats along with carefully delineated goals, objectives and classroom management lead to creative and productive learning in social studies.

PRACTICE EXERCISE

You are going to plan your future classroom and place the important things around it. For example the learning centers, where would you place them and how would you make them functional on a yearly basis? You are also exploring documents-based questions and need to create a document area where students have a constant supply of resources, a place to spread out and analyze their action-research data and do group work. You will also need a quiet reading area for students to spend time in. Think about all these things and begin to plot your ideal classroom.

REFLECTION EXERCISE

Now that you had created your dream-classroom, what are some problems you encountered? What are some problems you might anticipate having? For example, have you thought about circulation paths? Have you thought about operational rules so that your students self-regulate while working on their own? Have you decided how turn taking will take place? What if there is a real discipline problem? What if you run out of resources? What if your plan flops? These are all reality-based things that do happen. That is, why teachers plan, prepare, instruct and reflect, because there's no one-time happy medium. From one year to another, teachers refine what they do to make it more user-friendly, more productive and better and better every year.

Chapter Five

Ideal Classrooms & Self-regulated-learning

Chapter five explores the goals of teaching and learning in detail. The ideal classroom is designed to project the types of teaching and learning that will occur in our future classrooms. Classroom management principles are discussed as well as student engagement. Readers experience self-regulated learning.

THEORIES ON TEACHING AND LEARNING

So, we've had a glimpse into what our real teaching life will be like, provided we've planned and managed our design well. We've also been exposed to good teaching practices that can be imported into our classrooms. However, as I continuously tell you, our teaching is all about our students and not about us. So, forget about plans that appeal to you and instead, design learning opportunities that are motivating and inspirational for your students.

Our work in today's classrooms is for them and all about them. I insist on saying this because this is truly what multicultural education is all about. As instructors that realize that this is the true way, we move away from classical teaching environments, which were mainly autocratic, egocentric and ethnocentric. By this I mean, teacher-directed and teacher-centered. In the past, students were obedient followers of the teacher's design and plan. They carried out tasks that were necessary for them to evolve and to develop within a newly industrialized society. Today, our students evolve in a totally different era and operate in an entirely different world. They might actually know more about certain things than we do. Truly speaking, many youngsters cultivate a world of their own where many are no longer required to work and to help out their families, like in other centuries. The technology and the leisure time afforded youngsters today allows them to develop *dexterities* in areas that we have never had a chance to delve in. I'm speaking about the interactive games, the computerized world and the media.

Therefore, it behooves us to explore teaching environments that are supported by the kinds of things our students are interested in. Remember if we don't do this, we lose their focus of attention. I bet you many bored students can't wait to get out of these constricting classrooms and get back into their favorite *websites* or *chatrooms*. So, the message is loud and clear. Many young teachers are already doing this. They're asking their students what precisely they are interested in and incorporating these, of course, very selectively, adding interesting web-based information, media and technology into their daily teaching. To illustrate, one of my former graduate students became interested in a particular literary topic. To engage her students in the kinds of critical thinking she required she prepared slides based on familiar cartoons. Through this medium, the students elicited the kinds of dialogue that she wanted to help create for discussing literature in more depth.

To illustrate this in my own college lecture hall, I always bring out scenes from my favorite movie *Renaissance Man* starring Danny De Vito. If you've already seen the film, you might remember a scene where he requires all his students to bring a favorite book. He, being an English Major, brings Hamlet. His students, who are literacy-challenged school dropouts who've enlisted in the army, ask him to share excerpts from Hamlet with them. In response, and with the prevailing deficit orientation, which we all have to tune out of our system, he responds by saying, "It's too complicated. You won't understand."

A courageous and quite *savvy* student responds, "What, just because we didn't luck out on the good things in life you think we won't understand? Do you think we're stupid?" De Vito's character, realizes his mistake and begins to read Hamlet to the students very slowly, stopping to explain what is going on until the students begin to understand the universal issues involved. To make a story short, and for those who haven't seen the movie, De Vito creates an entire teaching/learning unit around these universal themes and the students respond quite well.

So, we've talked about the teacher-centered/ egocentric/ ethnocentric approach and realized that we all have a deficit-oriented background somewhere. As we learn to switch it off and to tune it out, we can move into a more student-centered-approach. As the graduate student did with familiar caricatures and Danny de Vito in the movie, we make things clear for our students so that they can relate with the big ideas in their very own way. We start slowly, with simple tasks and simple ideas and progressively weave in bigger topics and themes. Another former graduate student had another brilliant idea. As she taught about the Holocaust and Apartheid, she found *Rap* and *Hip Hop* songs that spoke about hate and violence. She had the students find them on the Internet, of course, with explicit precautions, etc. The students then were better able to understand the hatred implied in the prejudicial attitudes in both of these situations that seem so foreign to youngsters living in the United States today.

A common denominator that made both of these teaching/learning environments successful was that there were strong sets of rules in place. Students had very clear guidelines to follow. The teacher had precise and manageable goals. And, the instructional design was doable, inspirational and fun to do. These three concepts are key to any instructional design's success. Your leadership in the classroom is effective if you enforce (1) clear guidelines (2) manageable goals (3) interesting tasks. You wouldn't believe how engaged your students become and what little disciplining you have to do to keep the students motivated. However, you have to know a lot about self-regulation and how to enforce it in your classroom. I will describe this process in details next.

Self-regulation is a *classroom management* tool. Self-regulation leads to forward-moving, productive instruction. A self-regulated student knows exactly what he/she has to do and where to find the working tools and the information to get the task done. Self-regulation means less work for the teacher in the long-term, but requires lots of work and planning prior to implementation.

I've seen a self-regulated fifth grade classroom operate on its own for the three years that I observed it as a graduate student. The teacher set up certain classroom routines that managed themselves, literally. For example, she never had to indicate that it was *circle time* because once she moved towards the central carpet all students understood this signal and convened, in assigned seating spaces, around the teacher for carpet-based close instruction. At this point in time, the teacher brought out her small blackboard and read them their afternoon instructions. If the students had to carry out action research on their own, they went straight to the "action research" corner of the classroom where their individual clip-boards were arranged on a special shelf and in alphabetical order. They each took their clipboard and continued gathering data for their project.

Then without any bell or signal, they looked at the clock and knew that it was language arts time. So, they picked up their reading books in the reading corner and carried out whatever task they had to continue to do on their own. In this formidable classroom, I saw lots of things going on that any well-organized teacher can do. Of course, it was a centers-based classroom, which if well distributed, works well. But many of us will probably not have enough space or resources to have as many centers as we'd like. However, let me share some center-ideas that we all can do despite the many challenges we might face. None of these ideas require expensive furniture, space or materials so feel free to try them.

READING CORNER

When I had my classroom, I filled a laundry basket full of books, changing it each week or relating it to whichever theme I was teaching. At times, the school Librarian would provide me with special topic books, videos, listening tapes and other media. Beside the reading corner were the rules and expectations for all students to follow. For example, because the area was small, I only allowed three students to work there at one time. I usually had a set of pillows on the floor, a small rug, and perhaps three comfortable lounge chairs. Students could stay there and (1) read a book for pleasure, (2) conference about a book with peers (3) listen to a read-aloud story (4) watch a book-related video using earphones. You'd be amazed at how well behaved these students were. Why? When we show our students that we trust them with important materials and tasks then they don't need to manipulate us or to act silly. They respond by acting like the potential young adults that they are.

MAP CENTER

We don't do enough map-skill activity anymore in schools. You'd be surprised at how important these skills are and how much we use them on a daily basis. I would usually decorate this area with different kinds of maps and map-skill activities. I would also provide students with tracing paper and colors so that they could create their own maps. As a child myself, I used to love coloring maps, filling out the borders and penciling in the names of rivers, cities and towns. Because our social studies programs have left out a lot of these necessary skills and ideas, we need to supplement them through centers like these.

GAMES CENTER

Lots of important learning evolves from table games. In fact, in many cities of Canada, the game of chess is played in the classroom to develop logical-thinking skills in young people. As a Latina, I favor the game of dominoes. I teach it to all of my students because besides the basic mathematical strategies that I can teach through it, I can also reinforce the kinds of mental mathematics that is lacking in our mathematics programs. Again, a well-structured game center has its set of rules and clear goals. The students are to work in pairs. Often two pairs work best. In this way, one pair can drop out leaving an engaged pair still functionally operating within the games' guidelines. Students are responsible for setting-up and putting away game materials. They are to begin and complete a game prior to leaving the site. They are to exercise good sportsmanship, like in any game, and to respect one another. Popular games that all of my students have enjoyed can also help you disseminate multicultural ideas. For example, the popular "pick up sticks" is a Japanese game called *Mikado*. It consists in throwing a series of colored sticks and picking them up one by one without touching. The player who picks up the most sticks gains more points. *Mancala* is an African counting game. The board is designed much like the game of hopscotch and as the players make progress from one square to another they accumulate a certain amount of pebbles before moving forward. Dominoes are played worldwide and are very popular (I'd say a national sport) in many Spanish-speaking countries. I have met Arabic people who play it as well. It consists in matching numbered stones until players run out. The player who has matched all of his/her stones wins. All players have to mentally calculate how many stones are left and to strategically place their stones to win. As a mathematics educator, I've collected many more game ideas and provide them for you in the appendix.

ARTISTS' CORNER

This is perhaps the easiest center to upkeep. All you need is a desk, three chairs and recycled paper, colors, scissors and art materials. The rules for this center should be simple and clear, no more than three students working here at one time. They need to tidy up prior to leaving and once engaged in an art activity must conclude whatever they are doing to allow other students to enter. You don't want a lot of students floating around this center starting a project and leaving it half done. So, whoever engages in painting, cutting, pasting or drawing must engage in this activity for at least ten minutes prior to leaving. I would put a timer in the center and use it frequently. You could actually develop a rule whereby whosoever enters jots down his/her entry time, puts on the timer and leaves after the timer signals ten minutes.

CONVERSATION ROOM

You'd be surprised how effective this can be. The rules, again, should be manageable and simple. Turn taking is an important social task to learn. Students can engage in conversation without breaking the rules. The rule of thumb is, each person takes an item, holds it in his/her hand to begin talking and puts it down when done. In this way, everybody else listens to the entire piece without interrupting. Then, another person picks up the object, and releases it when done talking. I would suggest that no more than three people participate in the conversation corner at one time. The second rule is "indoor voices" which can be reinforced easily and rewarded as well. Only groups who have sustained indoor voices can use the conversation corner again, and so on.

MATHEMATHICS CORNER

There are all sorts of mathematical games that should be practiced outside of formal instructional time. Flash cards, money, counters and other manipulatives should be made available to students to reinforce skill-building activities. The more youngsters are exposed to mental math and logical thinking the better they will perform at any of these tasks. For this center, two people at a time are a good number. Hence, a more capable peer can teach multiplication and division skills to another student.

In the following part of this chapter, I'd like to share what an ideal classroom should look like. In my own view, I include what I found to be a very productive work place for youngsters as I quote from my book, *Children Solving Mathematical Problems* (Mellen House Press, 2003).

My Ideal Classroom

Elementary school classrooms today look and feel very different from ones that I taught in during the mid-seventies. Learning centers, computer stations, reading corners, and science activity centers appear here and there. Student artwork hangs from ceilings. Classroom pets strive for survival. Plants travel along walls. Student writing is published and displayed. Teachers bring a visiting library collection, along with children's publications to the author's corner. The designated author-of-the-day reads from the official author's chair. Classroom furniture is designed for group work and group activity. Students move around freely from a workstation to a learning center to the reading corner. Children are sprawled on the carpet, propped-up on a windowsill, under a desk—reading.

Children at Work

Ideally, youngsters in any classroom should be encouraged to:

seek out information, organize facts and ideas, communicate effectively both in speech and in writing, work independently or in cooperation with others, read with comprehension and enjoyment, and listen and think and read and write critically and creatively.

The ideal program that I witnessed as a graduate student is assessed on reading in content areas where the following skills are encouraged: (1) lan-

guage arts (2) critical thinking skills (3) map and global skills (4) graphic interpretation skills and (5) cooperative group work skills. They read several kinds of texts and genres and respond to readings either in a reader's log or by conferring with their teacher or peers. Children write daily, for diverse purposes and in a variety of formats, (journals, reading logs, creative genres, reports, etc.). They are asked to (1) organize ideas (2) express these with clarity (3) edit and revise (4) use writing conventions correctly (5) produce reader-appropriate texts.

The mathematics program has a problem-solving focus. Students are encouraged to (1) develop their thinking skills, (2) develop their ability to solve mathematical problems, (3) self-assess their needs. There is a clear demarcation between the conceptual (understanding of the problem) and the procedural (skills and operations). Children work with a textbook that emphasizes procedural skills' development. They are held accountable for knowing their tables and facts. However, they are also encouraged to think critically and to explore, use, and understand the mathematical concepts in more depth. They are provided a ninety-minute weekly problem-solving class where they work in small groups applying their skills and their abilities to solve real life mathematical problems.

A Problem-Solving Environment

Space is well distributed in this school. Environmental projects are cultivated as school-wide projects. Small play-fields and courts make room for an outdoor amphitheater, which blends the arts and sports masterfully. The main entrance is a problem-solving experience in and of itself. It is enlarged by a creative use of hallway mirrors, and a combination of colors pleasing the eye.

Wherever I look, I feel that somebody has solved a space problem with care and with a desire to maximize comfort. The teacher's lounge is a small, cozy room with fruit bowls laden with seasonal fresh fruit, a cookie jar with home-made snacks and freshly brewed tea and coffee. This welcoming teacher's lounge promotes a sharing and caring environment among the teachers avoiding inter-personal problems that often exist in schools.

Time-management is also a unique problem-solving feat. A lot of time is usually wasted in cloakrooms and hallways in many schools. Disputes usually arise when so many children are trying to do so much at once. However, this problem is cleverly addressed at the school and you will seldom see a tired teacher nagging at the children to move on to the playground so that she can catch her morning coffee. On the contrary, the meal-monitor takes over this duty for the teacher.

The children come and go freely in this small classroom. They do not bump into each other or get into each other's way. They work well together using *appropriate vocabulary and applying appropriate writing skills that allow them to articulate explanations (in both verbal and written form.) They have learned to cultivate writing as an art form, enjoying reading and writing in different genres during their Language Arts program. They have also learned to speak to each other politely and to respect their differences. For example, most students speak up and speak out if they want to. They are not restrained or constrained by classroom rules that limit their verbal interactions. However, I rarely over-heard children speaking to each other in a derogatory fashion or using rude, loud language. Students are free to come and go without having to sign out or ask permission. Although classroom space is reduced, students move around without much confusion and noise. The requirements of the problem-solving program in mathematics are such that students must read, write, and talk about mathematics in real contexts using real examples and tangible objects.*

So from this example, you can see that self-regulation can work. If you plan your centers and your classroom so as to include your students in your planning, they will feel included and will respond well. If you structure things so that you can manage them with ease, then it will work. However, don't try anything that you don't feel comfortable doing. If you do plan to implement any of these ideas, start slowly and begin small. You can't run all of these centers at once if you've never done this before. So, I recommend much caution because all of these wonderful ideas can flop if not done properly.

Back to the concept of a self-regulated student and a classroom where students are independent of the teacher, it takes lots of clarity and good planning! If you have clear guidelines and you address the issues that you anticipate ahead of time, then your self-regulated classroom will run smoothly. When I say anticipate I mean knowing about and anticipating what you might do in the event that certain things "might happen". Good planning requires anticipating problems. Just like the caregiver that ensures that the child is properly clothed prior to going out in cold or hot weather, the teacher anticipates the following:

1. Relational problems amongst students: some students don't and won't get along no matter how you try. So, how are you going to avoid conflict?
2. Circulation problems: you need to create space so that you are not confined by the centers you create. This requires paper and pencil planning so that you create a circulation plan for "crowd control" purposes.
3. Organizational issues: you might want to prioritize, catalogue and organize materials so that you have easy access to them. Just like the Librarian, who always finds what she needs on whichever shelf it was assigned to,

you can duplicate this model in your classroom so, if the object isn't there when you need it, either somebody has it or you have to replace it with a new one.

4. Communication. You need to have predictable routines whereby you inform your students of what is going on, what you expect of them and what they will be required to do. Circle time is always a good time for that as students are relaxed, seated on a carpet and you are addressing them informally. You might also address their non-self-regulation privately and in writing. A journal is a good spot to reprimand or discipline a student without embarrassing him/her in public. It is also a good communication tool between you, the child and his/her parents. Inter-student communication is also important. Children learn a lot by talking to and listening to others. You should create space and time for this. Finally, school-home communication is a key to best teaching practices. We need to align the care-providers to our cause. We need to invite them to join us in the classroom whenever possible. And please, when you need to discuss a child's progress, invite the child into this event. Have a conference between you, the parents and the child. Sometimes many things that could be settled out of court are settled with ease with this brief meeting.

So what is a self-regulated learner like? This is a learner who knows where to be at every moment he/she is in your care. It is also an intellectualy-engaged learner who is really present in all of the tasks he/she needs to do. It's like a job. The student checks in, does his/her work, checks out and goes home. You, the teacher, are there to orient, facilitate, distribute materials, tasks and learning formats, and to communicate with your students. They are in your care to (1) acquire and perfect skills (2) gather and interpret data (3) develop and enhance their literacy (4) communicate with each other and you (5) take charge of their own learning.

If you need to *ham up* the learning experiences for them by having them don learning caps, aprons, clip-boards, magnifying glasses and other props to learn, well so-be-it, do it. Nothing like a scene from another favorite of my films, *Stand and Deliver* where *Edward James Olmos* dons a street-vendor's hotdog cap, an apron and a machete to chop an apple into parts. He uses this stunt to engage his student in logical thinking. As he moves around the classroom asking students how much they learn that percents and decimals are related and that parts belong to a whole. This is the spice of teaching and learning, doing whatever is in your power to get the job done. A good sense of humor goes far. Sometimes a silly little stunt like this one clarifies a confusing concept. In actual fact, this movie is based on a true story where *Jaime Escalante,* a Bolivian computer/mathematics specialist prepared a group of high school drop outs for Advanced Placements Mathematics. He was so successful in preparing them for the exam that the authorities, in disbelief accused him of cheating. A court case evolved and the issue was resolved as the students excelled in the test a second time.

On the other hand, if everything is going well, you need to praise your students and to celebrate their progress. To illustrate, an old friend of mine established what she called coffee break she had brought in an old dining room set into her classroom, populated it with teacups, etc., and created a celebratory space for her students.

Once they had successfully completed a task, they were given coffee break tickets that they could redeem at the end of the week. So, on Friday's she would provide milk and cookies for coffee break time and the children would conclude their week happily.

I instituted a special lunch time treat for my students. Back in the 1980's, when I taught fourth grade, I worked very hard at setting up my group-work activities. It took a lot of effort on my part to make, enforce and distribute the kinds of learning environments that I needed and I rallied student-support by celebrating with each group who showed self-regulatory behavior successfully. Therefore, at the end of each week, I would invite them to lunch. They loved having lunch with their teacher. We ate all sorts of finger food that they liked and partied together. Because this was a rotational activity, the other students knew that their turn was soon due and there were no hard feelings.

My recommendation is that once you expect self-regulated behavior from your students, you begin to move away from the reward system and simply expect students to be at their most adult, relaxed, receptive learning modes at all times. You can build this environment by communicating with them, reading and responding to their journal queries and simply telling them how you expect them to carry out the tasks they need to work on independently.

To illustrate, the fifth grade teacher that I observed during my doctoral studies had all sorts of communication devices for her students. If she wanted them to study their math skills on their own, she would post the tasks, the schedule for doing these and the expected outcomes in the mathematics corner. Students did this on their own without having to be told to do this. They had an itemized list of tasks to complete and checked them off one by one. If she wanted them to peruse her newest book basket, she would provide different colored post-it notes for them to give her feedback. So, a child would peruse a book post a yellow, blue or pink note on the back page indicating his/her rating. When all the books had been rated, she would then create another reading-related activity based on the students' preferences. She would read their journals on a weekly basis and in this way check up on them to see what tasks they had completed and which tasks they would need to complete for the next week. So, the school as a job environment was set up and it provided the self-regulatory behavior this teacher expected from all of her students.

Should you or would you be able to establish this system? This is a good question for you to ponder on your own. My advice is for you to try things that work for you. One can't import everybody else's plan into one's life. Much in the same way that we can't inhabit other people's lives, we shouldn't feel like the more senior educators should tell us how and what to do in our classrooms. We should, however, try things that we like and that we know we can sustain.

PRACTICE EXERCISE: SELF-REGULATED LEARNING.

Now that you have been exposed to centers-based instruction and self-regulated learning, it's a good opportunity to devise your own classroom rules and your own expectations for self-regulated learning. Use the above templates to plan for and anticipate scenarios in hour future classroom.

REFLECTION EXERCISE

Having read about all of this exciting stuff and perhaps delved a bit into your own ideal classroom planning, it's a good moment to stop and to reflect on your past experiences and their impact on your future classroom. Perhaps you had a teacher who taught you in this way. Maybe you could jot down your memories of this positive experience and in so doing remember what went well and didn't go so well. You might also reflect on the contrary, a teacher who had you so constricted that you had little room to move. Reflect on these and use your reflections for your future classroom design.

Chapter Six

Connected & Integrated Learning

Chapter six introduces instructional ideas that connect and integrate learning. The *thematic unit, lesson plans, rubrics, and pre-teaching/post-teaching activities* are explored in great depth. Readers draft a thematic unit of their own.

THEORIES ON INSTRUCTIONAL PLANNING

I find that knowing where I'm going and what I'm going to do when I get there gives me a blueprint for planning my actions. I also find it hard to start planning before I know where I'm going. I therefore suggest a format that has worked for me in my elementary school classroom.

Using Rubrics

I like to start with a rubric. This is a tool used by many teachers to focus on the task itself and to simplify instructions to students. To introduce a rubric-based forum for learners, I use a simple two-step rubric. The rubric looks like this:

Task	Date	Student
Completed successfully		In progress

In this simple way and by using this format, you can help the student regulate his/progress. He/she will simply give you an update of the status of the task and you will indicate what needs to be done. You've got the task at hand, the date in which it was updated and your immediate feedback. Depending on what it is you are going to teach students, and always keeping in mind that a rubric is a tool for you to guide them as they regulate their own learning, you can use a three four column rubric later on. To illustrate, here's a sample rubric for a Language Arts composition:

RUBRIC FOR COMPOSITION

Name of Student

As you can tell, there's numeric feedback, in other words, the students is producing (4) excellent work or (1) work that needs more attention. I always like to focus on the positive. Therefore, you will notice that I have given the student credit for having done the work. Some rubrics don't do this and assign students a failing grade of *0*. I wouldn't encourage that. Rather, I'd like students to work their way up from a one to a four if possible by submitting multiple drafts.

So, a rubric can be developed for any classroom format and for any topic of choice. You will have an opportunity to design your own in the practice portion of this chapter. I've included sample rubrics in the appendix for your perusal.

PRE & POST-TEACHING ACTIVITIES

For this second phase of the teaching/learning process, I suggest generating pre-teaching and post-teaching activities. These activities involve finding out what the students need to learn and whether we have successfully taught them the needed skills. Teachers use various forms of assessment during the learning process. We all engage in some form of checking system to direct our teaching. I suggest a formal system so that we teach what we need to teach and resolve pending learning gaps successfully. As with the rubric, pre and post-teaching activities are designed around our basic teaching needs. Hence, we should survey our students prior to teaching them something new before actually engaging in the teaching. Some of us already do this all the time. We ask questions and informally find out what our students already know before becoming redundant. I suggest that any pre/post teaching activity become a routine for you in every class you teach.

You are very familiar with this context as we do it all the time in our real lives. We like to find out who we are meeting and what it is we are doing in any new situation, right? So, how about doing this with your students? I suggest you look at what you are going to teach for the day, or lesson, and stop for a minute to generate a few questions about it. As you begin teaching, you gauge what your students know about the topic and what you need to teach them. In doing so, I'm sure you'll scratch off a few items from your teaching list and add items you hadn't thought about. Also, why teach things your students already know? So with a few probing questions and a nice wrap-up at the end, your lessons should flow evenly and smoothly.

A simple rule of thumb in pre-teaching is to assess knowledge. In mathematics, for example, teachers might give students the end-of-chapter exam to

1	2	3	4
Needs more work	Satisfactory	Very satisfactory	Outstanding
Proof-read Add info Redo	Good punctuation needs ideas	Good punctuation Excellent ideas Reads very well	Super punctuation Superb
Draft 1 Draft 2 Draft 3			

find out what they already know. Depending upon their responses, you will be able to gauge what to focus on during your teaching. In other topics, this is harder to do. So I suggest that your pre-teaching activities which are tailored around the initial information you need to provide your students. In a social studies unit, you might generate questions that situate the learners in the era and context of the historical moment you will be teaching them about. Your classroom time-line will come in handy to elicit questions and answers about the surrounding events of the era. In a language arts lesson, where students are to write a composition, you might revisit their lexical and semantic knowledge as well as provide a review of the grammar and punctuation you'd want them to use.

In any other area, depending upon your lesson plan and teaching objectives, you'll use these pre-teaching opportunities for review. In terms of post-teaching, again, you'll gauge the outcomes of your teaching efforts by a pop-quiz, questionnaire, or survey demonstrating that your students are using the newly acquired knowledge. You might again plan ahead, view your goals and objectives and match these to the outcomes of your teaching. The post-teaching activities that you end up teaching once you've gauged the learning should solidify these newly acquired learning pieces so that you can move on to newer learning.

In mathematics, you might provide the end-of-chapter test again to see if the students are now able to answer all the questions. If they don't, then concentrate on re-teaching the needed concepts and don't spend time duplicating redundant topics and skills. In other areas, like language arts, for example, multiple-drafts and entries provide you with opportunities to encourage progress and growth. In social studies, students are either: (1) able to recognize facts and issues or (2) able to relate these within a context. So, if your students are only at stage one, you need to bring them to stage two. Exposure, opportunities to speak about what they have learned and life-like situations where they can almost tell you what went on historically as they converse, will provide them with the re-teaching/learning opportunities needed.

To illustrate from my own personal teaching/learning life, my English teacher had us prepare creative book-reports. In so doing, we not only situated our audience within the plot, setting and characters, but also within a context. We hence had to resort to our history and geography skills to relate the book to historical events. So, when we talked about such books as *Little Women* or *Of Mice & Men* we had to include information about the Civil War, for the Louisa May Alcott book, or information on the situation of migrant farm workers in John Steinbeck's narrative. Hence, we had to do a little bit of research and self-actualization in order to sound knowledgeable and thorough. This is not a difficult task to expect from your students, as you can expect this kind of knowledge-construction to happen in any subject. As I've frequently said, learning cannot occur in a vacuum. Students need to relate what they are learning and to situate it within a context that works for them. If you create an appealing, exciting learning scenario where your students will be proud presenters of these contexts, you will solidify their learning. Again, all of this happens under good construction and planning. Here's how to go about it.

THE SIMPLE LESSON PLAN

Usually, pre-service teachers squirm when they hear the words "lesson plan". They think that writing a lesson plan is the hardest task ahead of them. Let me tell you that if you apply a simple formula your task will be very easy. I use the following format: (1) rubric (2) pre/post teaching and (3) what they need to learn. Hence, as I've said before, I begin by writing out my goals and objectives. Then I plan a simple rubric and then I generate the lesson plan tailored around my needs. You might wonder how all of this can happen if you're up there in front of the room teaching. Most of the time, we are not providing formal instruction in the classroom. Much of the time we are guiding and assessing our students. If you feel uncomfortable over days when you are not following a strict plan or guideline, you can jot down in your planbook that you are carrying out formal pre-instructional activities.

This is considered valid instruction in my book. This might take up half a morning or the first couple of days of the week. That is all right. It's like priming the wood you are working on in your tool-shed or scraping off the old layer of varnish prior to re-painting something. The preparative portion of the teaching/learning experiences is considered valid teaching/learning activity. So, you've gauged your learners and you know what you need to teach them. That's what you write down in your lesson plan.

So, what do you need to include in your lesson plan? One, you need to start with a goal/objective (what you are going to teach). Next you need to gather the instruments and materials you will need to teach that relate to this topic (realia, documents, artifacts, etc.) Finally, you will need to gauge your time so that you have enough time to develop your ideas.

That's all you need to teach a lesson well. So, if you begin with a good set of probing questions, you plan what you will bring and do, and you wrap up the lesson with a good idea of what you taught effectively, you will have delivered a good lesson.

We haven't brought up the *S* word. Yes, S = Standards. You do have to include the standards that you will be meeting in your written blueprint. Most states expect all teachers to use the instructional standards and to meet curricular constraints of this kind. I suggest you keep a list of the ones that belong to your teaching discipline or domain so that you always know which standards you are meeting in your teaching. Once you have done these several times the task becomes easier.

Some of my pre-service teachers fret over the length of their lesson plans. I prefer the short and sweet kind. These should include a brief outline of all of what you will be exploring in a given lesson. Some plans lead into each other. For this purpose, you might want to break them up into time slots or teaching days.

Ultimately, you will never do everything you've written on your lesson plan. However, over-planning is always key to a good lesson. You can never predict what your students will say or do in your classroom. So, it's always good to be prepared.

So here's the simple formula:

1. Goal (to teach about the Age of Discovery)
2. Objective (to have students relate this era to Columbus and other explorers)
3. Standards to be met (geography skills, historical topics, etc.)
4. Pre-teaching questions (what led to the Age of Exploration, who were the key players during this era, what was the role of the monarchy, what were some inventions that helped solidify exploration, etc.)
5. Realia needs (photographs, maps, travel instruments, samples of spices, etc.)
6. What you will teach (the truth . . . within a solid contextual framework)
7. How you will teach it (through story-telling, videos, several points of view, real documents, personal narratives, etc.)
8. What will the students do (read, discuss, collect, write, explore on their own, narrate, etc.)
9. How you will assess this (final project)

PRACTICE EXERCISE

For this portion of the chapter, you will practice writing a rubric, pre/post teaching activities and a model lesson plan. You can use the format I've provided or create your own. Take our time to do this well and to feel comfortable with the process. I would like you to jot down the questions, doubts and thoughts you had while doing this.

_____

_____

_____

_____

RUBRIC

Practice developing a rubric of your own. I use a simple table and fill it in. Usually, the less you put on the rubric the better. Remember, you are the one correcting these, so you don't want to be overwhelmed with too many things to look for in each of the @25 papers you will be grading with the rubric. Start with a simple table:

_____

_____

_____

_____

Then fill it in with what you want your students to do. Remember you don't
want to discourage your students, so start with an easy plan.

Again, you tailor this to your needs. If you're doing a science lab, you might
want to specify what it is you want your students to do in the lab. If you're
teaching a skill direct the learning by specifying which skill your are grading.
Enjoy creating your own rubric.

PRE & POST TEACHING ACTIVITIES:

Remember, if you know where you're going, you will certainly get there.
However, if you don't have a clear plan or route, you'll have trouble. So, I encourage teachers to plan ahead carefully and to prepare their students early
on. I like to plan a lesson by (1) gauging where the students are at, and (2)
measuring how far they went through my teaching. So, I design pre and post
teaching activities to gauge and measure. Pre-teaching activities could be a
series of three to five questions about what you're going to teach and post-
teaching activities could be these same three to five questions with additional
information added. In this way you could find out if all of your students
learned what you intended to teach them. Try this out for yourselves and test
some of this as you go along.

LESSON PLAN FORMAT:

Again, I use a simple format and keep in mind where it is I want to go at
all times. I encourage you to try this as you plan your lessons. Remember
you have a lot of things to think about, so pack your lesson well before-
hand. A good rule of thumb is this simple format I provide here. Enjoy
planning.

Title of your lesson:

Goals you plan to attain:

Realia you will need to bring:

Standards to be met:

What will your students be doing:

Time allocated for each task:

Extensions and follow-through ideas:

REFLECTION EXERCISE

Now that you've planned, assessed and measure the learning, please take the time to reflect on what we have covered and how you will incorporate these ideas into your practice.

Chapter Seven

Student-engagement & Individualized Instruction

Chapter seven focuses on the academically engaged student and what he/she is encouraged to do in a multicultural classroom. Action research, data-informed learning, evidence-based instruction, and the use of *realia* to enhance learning are explored. Readers explore individualized instruction.

THEORIES ON STUDENT ENGAGEMENT

An academically engaged student is one who is excited about what he/she is doing in the classroom. This student has a keen sense of agency as he/she continues to develop an idea, to manufacture a product for display, to interview people for a survey, or to solve a problem. The student is lost in his/her creative endeavor and anticipating an ultimate outcome, which might be very gratifying. There is a wonderful sense of satisfaction as ideas are explored and shared with others. This type of ideal learning environment is product and process-oriented. Students are their own change agents as they defend a point of view, provide feedback to others and generate new ideas. Ideally, this type of instructional setting can be managed and organized by any teacher.

The excitement of such academic engagement happens in well-designed classrooms where there is sufficient time for exploration and lots of mobility. Teachers who develop year-round time-lines, learning centers, data-gathering opportunities and discursive forums of exploration for their students will encourage and promote this type of engaged activity. As the agents of change that we have become, teachers are now busy compiling information, brokering and negotiating time frames for students to leave the classroom and to present their findings elsewhere.

To illustrate, I will walk you through the kinds of learning environments I mean (action research, data-informed learning, evidence-based instruction, using realia.) As the teacher that you are, you broker and negotiate desirable learning environments for your students. You are an agent of change as you select contemporary, actualized and dynamic instructional materials. Your students are able to watch how you deal with things, manage instruction, and orient their learning. As the change agent that you are, your decisions become transparent behavior models for them. Ultimately, they will follow your lead if you show them the way. So, as you hand down your wisdom, don't be afraid to transparently share your doubts, thoughts and ideas. You pave the way for them through your example. They too become brokers, negotiators and change agents. Your job is to provide them with the tools and the opportunities to engage in this highly productive behavior.

I have already mentioned some props that I enjoy using to generate the inquisitive type of behavior I will describe shortly. As I have said in previous chapters, don't hesitate to acquire the types of gadgets and props that will get the job done. One of my favorite activities is that of the detective work required in research. I enjoy sharing my own research-informed processes with my students. As I share the ways I collect and interpret data, I pave the way for them to do their own. I will describe these formats separately.

ACTION RESEARCH

In the area of mathematics, most states embrace a data-gathering/data-analyzing process as one of their required standards. This requires students to seek their own information and to interpret their findings. In order to do this in my classroom, I buy individual clipboards for each of my students, store them in an accessible spot in the classroom and generate survey or questionnaire tablets for them to do this exercise frequently. I try to make this a bi-weekly process so that the habit of collecting, summarizing and interpreting is formed.

Ideas that you can use to involve students in this type of action research are multiple. You might like to relate your activities to school-based processes. Your students can survey students in their grade, floor, level, etc., over cafeteria food preferences. They can ask their peers whether they prefer fresh salads over steamed vegetables. Then, once they tally their data, they can actually produce change in their school lives. The interesting thing about action research is that it is fun to do, highly manageable, given you've clarified your rules and expectations, and very productive. Your students practice their mathematics skills with a direct product that can be interpreted and used in their favor.

A related topic that may come forth as they report their data is that their analysis might result in a newsletter article or report. Language arts and mathematics are now directly involved and the students are doing something that they can handle themselves. If you'd like to see the applications in other subject areas, take for example science. You might have them investigate the benefits of steamed vegetables over fresh salads. When they come up with their scientifically based results, they can make solid recommendations based on real evidence.

Action research can benefit students in multiple ways. Dialogue, discussion and structured scenarios evolve allowing students to engage in their own pursuit. The more reserved, quiet student will learn to engage in free conversation with others while the outgoing student will also benefit. Students will learn to talk to each other and to listen to each other. As communication improves, so do their thinking processes. You'd be surprised at how things change when students become vocal about things that interest them.

DATA-INFORMED LEARNING

You have seen in the examples I've provided above, that an implicated, present, totally engaged student will fight for something he/she feels ownership about. Data-informed learning takes a life of its own as student's points of view emerge and shape their conversations. Data-informed learning is empowering.

Aside from survey and questionnaire data, students can work on the Internet, gathering true data on sports, the evolution of a journalistic story, or any real issue they are interested in. You can discuss the safety guidelines with your students and keep track of the web-sites they are visiting. You should also make it very clear that the consequences for unacceptable behavior are severe and that you will take necessary action if your students stray from your instructions. Once you've covered this area of intrigue with both your students and their parents, you can proceed to work with data-informed learning.

When I discussed learning centers, I mentioned a graduate student of mine who generates learning environments from web-sites. She collects sites that intrigue her and her students and allows them to make their own explorations and connections. At this point in time and this day and age, I wouldn't discourage you from using music, elements of popular culture and cultural icons that appeal to your students. You have already established the safety precautions and ground rules that you need. Your students are not going to stray from your guidance. So let them find out what their favorite rap artist or movie celebrity are doing as socially engaged individuals. I for one am a proud fan of Bono (U2) and Sting. They are very engaged in world issues. As my students guide and facilitator, I would present my own collection of data-informed material on these celebrities' involvement as a starting point.

Some of your students might want to talk about their favorite athletes as well. Many football and basketball stars have literacy programs or sports programs they support to help underrepresented youth. Role models like these are excellent data-informed study material.

Other areas that I like to tune into are gender-based ones where I take advantage of this learning forum to plug my female heroes. Girls need to see that there were important women in history who were scientists, mathematicians and change agents. They also have to become acquainted with socially engaged women dealing with today's issues.

EVIDENCE-BASED INSTRUCTION

I've coined this phrase inspired by what in the social studies arena is referred to as *document-based questions*. Inspired by this format I feel that students can become engaged, self-regulated learners as they read and learn about real things in real settings. Therefore, as you teach them anything they need to learn, you have them relate what they are learning to a real application in life. So, you avoid having your students learn in a vacuum.

With this in mind, let us begin with my favorite topic, mathematics. If your students are learning about decimals and percents, remember to give them a true-life application so that they can apply it to a life-like task. Have them find out where the whole decimal system originated and the controversy behind adopting it. As they find the evidence, they begin to understand the concept holistically.

In the areas of social studies, science and language arts, your imagination should provide you with the leads, the quests, and the leadership you will need to engage your students in their own search for the truth. My two favorite topics, the Age of Exploration and Immigration can become focal points for you to tell and interpret the colonization process in America. Couched in real data and true information, your students can generate value-laden reports about how this process evolved.

You will certainly replace the misconceived stories they've been told about Columbus, the First Thanksgiving and a myriad others. I recommend you choose one topic, develop it fully and carry it out through the entire academic year. Start collecting materials, data, mementos, clippings, photographs and the kinds of things that will help you provide a more realistic learning forum for your students.

Chapter Seven

REALIA

Nothing is more exciting than to view a film, to scan through a collection of photographs or to read the letters written by historical protagonists. Realia is all of these things and more. It's the hands-on building blocks of learning. Handling real manipulatives or replicas of what you are learning about makes the learning more real. The word realia, borrowed from Librarian-speak means exactly that, anything that is real, yet transportable and manageable in the classroom.

Have a store in your classroom. Provide your students with shopping opportunities where dealing with real money converts them into wise consumers. Bring mementos, souvenirs, replicas of items you talk about, so that they can experience them. Trust your students so that in the handling of these objects there are moments for sharing and for storing. You will be surprised with the outcomes.

PRACTICE EXERCISE

Take some time to practice some of the ideas included in this chapter.

REFLECTION EXERCISE

Now that you have worked in this way, find some time to reflect on what you have gleaned so far.

The Transformation Process

Chapter eight focuses on James Banks' transformation model. Readers have explored self and other as well as instructional scenarios. They have also spent time in a real classroom. At this point in time, mid-semester, they should also be experiencing some form of transformation. Readers explore the concept of teacher as broker, negotiator, informer and change agent. Readers role-play.

THEORIES ON MULTICULTURAL TRANSFORMATION

James Banks, in his book Cultural Diversity in Education (2001) talks about the kinds of engagement multicultural educators have to consider as they join those of us who have been teaching this for a number of years. He believes that for a successfully integrated Multicultural Education Program to exist in schools today, it has to come from a joint effort that includes the entire staff, administration and educational community.

This calls for a complete overhaul of our schools, our teaching, and our learning environment. Historically, when it comes to integrating multicultural concepts into our classrooms, educators and the educational community engaged in what Banks calls a level one, *contributions approach*. This approach leads school administrators and the community at large to allow teachers to include cultural events around the school, which focus on sporadic celebrations. Hence such iconic heroes as *Sacajawea, Squanto, Lewis & Clark*, and others are placed in the foreground temporarily. Their exploits and contributions are celebrated and mystified. Sometimes, as well, certain excitable holidays were also included to diversify the already over-celebrated ones in existence.

Soon, however, certain sociopolitical events that permeated society historically caused movements leading to a conscience-awareness and awakening.
People in general and teachers in the classroom began to add to the contributions of these heroes and heroines and now included what Banks considers to
be a level two or additive approach. This level permitted the inclusion of discussions, for example of *Rosa Parks* or *Martin Luther King*, and subsequently
a *Black History Month* was scheduled into the social calendar of many
schools and colleges. Other additions to the calendar were made without
changing or modifying anything of what was being taught.

Subsequently, with a few of these additions, and a little conscious awakening we reached a level three or transformation approach. Some serious thinking was starting to happen, leading to a need for modifying what we taught
and discussed in class. This gradual change allowed for more space in the
classroom itinerary for teachers. Those who had access to the Internet and
other resources were able to integrate online data-collecting activities for
their students to explore. Documents and artifacts were made accessible to
students and teachers so they could explore the truth and enrich their teaching and learning. At this point in time, the revolution of the Internet allowed
for the truth to surface clearly in front of our eyes. Our students, prompted by
the document-based nature of certain instructional subjects were now navigating through as much truth as they could muster to question what they were
being taught. The transformation also bred more authentic dialogue between
teachers and students, leading to a new wave in instruction.

The fourth level, social action approach is perhaps the most difficult to
achieve in schools today. It requires a concerted effort from teachers and students to act upon what they think needs to be modified in the world around
them. Teachers should find ways, as the agents of change that they are, to
reach out to the community that they serve and to provide a forum of ex-
change that will connect the school to the community that hosts them. Educators, administrators, students, and the community should engage in dialogue, cultural exchanges and shared celebrations of what really matters and
cultural links that set the mood for real partnerships.

I say that this is hard to do for many reasons. Research informs us that
many teachers do not reside in the area where they are teaching. Much like
the bussing program of the 1950's and 1960's, teachers are also *bussed* to
schools. Teachers who don't live within their teaching communities cannot
have the same impact on their educational arena. It's so plain and simple.
They don't participate in the academic, cultural and sports activities that occur after school hours. They don't get to see their students excel in other areas like gymnastics, acting, track & field and competitive sports. They don't
see the students delivering papers or running car-washes or all of these other

community-based opportunities that also teach them how to be functional and deserving citizens.

I am sounding a bit preachy here, but shouldn't we move in with our own constituents? Wouldn't it be nicer to plan our lives around those of our students? I am proud to say that as multicultural educator, I have gotten more satisfaction from supporting my higher education students through their intermural activities, college games, shows and fund-raisers. Being a visible, caring member has earned me the respect and credibility I need to continue bearing the torch of multicultural education. Because I go to events and am totally immersed in what goes on in my educational community, I am more informed, enriched and well rounded. I often tailor what I teach around what I experience.

Therefore, I exhort other educators to join me in this participatory crusade. It is well worth your while if you envision teaching for the next twenty or thirty years. The other piece of advice I offer is to be a respectable citizen wherever you are and whomever you are with. Educators are highly visible individuals. There are unspoken social rules and norms we need to abide by in public. A quick reminder or rule of thumb, don't let down your guard at any time.

PRACTICE EXERCISE

Take some time to reflect on these ideas.

REFLECTION EXERCISE

Chapter Nine

Empathy, Equity & Excellence

Chapter nine focuses on the three E's: *empathy, equity and excellence*. Legislation, the legacies of *Brown vs. Board* and *Lau vs. Nichols* as well as the mandates of the *No Child Left Behind Act* are put in a multicultural perspective. Readers re-enact some of these court cases. Theories on equity, excellence, and clarity have now become multicultural mandates. The goals of multicultural education present this concept as insights about (1) what is happening in today's schools and classrooms (2) how these issues are addressed or ignored and (3) the many language barriers that occur as parallel instruction, popular culture and even a culture of power in school settings. Critical thinking and learning go hand in hand when all three components are present (equity, excellence and clarity). Learners are treated fairly. They are expected to perform to their highest potential and to perform well at whatever tasks they are expected to do. We provide them with the necessary tools, with an adequate learning environment and with best practices in teaching so that this goal is met.

The population of learners we are seeing in our schools and universities is rapidly changing. Impressive demographic charts would be pointless to show you the changes in today's classrooms. Not only are demographics in today's classrooms changing, but the many vernaculars, jargons and discipline-specific languages shared among participants changing.

Often, students and teachers speak totally different languages and in fact, live in very different worlds. Jim Cummins at the last NABE and TESOL Conferences explored the topic of language acquisition and the battle for instituting Bilingual Education Programs throughout America. He spoke about the positive influence that second and third-language acquisition plays on an individual, allowing the person to have a broader perspective on life and eventually to negotiate with realities in stereo or even tri-dimensional versions. He also spoke about the importance of developing academic discourse in today's classrooms (elementary to post-secondary) in an effort to raise the register and to use more specific language. Ultimately, Cummins urged his audience to realize the importance of vocabulary development in their teaching and proposed lots of interaction with discipline-specific words as a resource. Of course integrating lots of reading, integrating new genres and promoting literacy, continue to be key obligations for all teachers.

We can attempt to do all of that and be very successful as individuals and as instructors. But, we need to remember that learners and interlocutors alike are processing information at a different rate than the speaker/instructor and are negotiating and juggling contexts, text, content, and realities in their very own way. Teach better, use more exciting learning tools and change school directions so that learning is more relevant for everybody. But how is this done and what strategies can we do to achieve these goals?

One way is, of course, to raise discourse patterns, the registers in which we speak so that our students are dealing with more complex ideas. We should elevate the use of more desirable vocabulary in hopes of promoting analytical/critical thinking and ultimately synthesis of knowledge, the top wrung on Bloom's taxonomy.

But, we cannot do this if there is little or no engagement in the classroom and information is not delivered without clarity of delivery and purpose. We already know that often, students sit in classes for countless hours wondering what the purpose of a class is or what direction the speaker is taking. Technology offers us wonderful resources and support systems to assist us in presenting ideas and delivering instruction. But, the ultimate goal is communication. I use Stephen Cary's book *Second Language Learners* (1997) on teaching the second language learner to teach my pre-service teachers how to manufacture good instructional tools that are (1) simple (2) well-thought out (3) engaging enough that students want to perform the tasks and (4) accountable.

We cannot teach without a good plan, a good assessment tool of what we've taught, and inevitably, performance of a desirable task. Cary encourages us to include and teach all learners as if they were learning something for the first time. Besides using clear tools and instructional devices, he recommends that we too invest some time and effort in our work so that we are enjoying the process!

We need to teach material in formats that are amenable to the learners and exciting for ourselves as well? We can experiment with different avenues for the learning to be delivered in a palatable fashion. But, always remembering that it's about students and not about us.

Isn't it true, that sometimes, we get carried away entertaining our students and enjoying being the people-in-charge. Tuning into our students and how they are perceiving, and performing remains of utmost importance. The lens of multicultural education provides me with another valuable tool.

I have adopted Valerie Ooka Pang's *caring-centered approach*, which talks about nurturing the learner, believing in the learner, and promoting learning through a personal investment. My own multicultural perspective and the way that I make meaning helps me tune into the needs of my students and ultimately the task at hand.

James A. Banks talks about educational reform as a tool for change in the public educational system of the United States. The term equity appears more and more in the literature. Elevating the expectations for students and again, elevating discourse patterns, transactions with texts, and ultimately the registers of speech in which students are working in are important concepts that we've always known. Working at the top of Bloom's taxonomy is an empowering mantra that we attempt to say as we teach our university courses.

These are good questions. We hope that the answers are positive and in favor of most of our students. The bell curve lingers above us informing us that there will always be students who are (1) not well served (2) falling through the cracks (3) really not with the program.

On the other hand, we are supposed to spread the learning to make it more equitable. How do we do that? Paulo Freire says that:

1. *Education is not neutral*: It liberates the individual to become a proactive, critical thinker.
2. *Content comes from participants*. Issues become relevant when the learner is invested in
3. *Promoting dialogue*. Dialogue to share views establishes communication.
4. *Creating a problem-posing learning atmosphere*. Invested learners generate interesting questions and solutions.
5. *Making room for reflection/action*. Reflection leads to action, which in turn creates research.
6. *Encouraging Transformation*. Enlightened students move forward.

PRACTICE EXERCISE

_____

_____

_____

_____

_____

REFLECTION EXERCISE

_____

_____

_____

_____

_____

Chapter Ten

The Essence of
Multicultural Education

Chapter ten recaptures the essence of multicultural education in light of the personal transformation, teaching and learning styles, actualized information, and the mission we have ahead of us. Readers generate their own goals for multicultural education in their future classrooms.

THEORIES ON DESIGN FOR CROSS-CULTURAL LEARNING

We have been wrongly taught to assume that people of another culture or sub-culture see, feel, and think the way we do. It is true that certain basic emotions, such as joy and sorrow, are common to all cultures. But the ways of expressing these feelings may not be the same. The majority of well-educated people have a passive understanding of other cultures. An active understanding requires experience. An active understanding also requires the development of gut level attitudes and reactions that demonstrate an acceptance of others. This means, demonstrating that one has respect for and a tolerance threshold for cultural differences. These cannot always be attained in the classroom setting which is highly artificial and appealing to the intellect. We can, however, talk to our students about examples of these gut level attitudes and reactions to instill in them an understanding that we need to teach and be taught tolerance.

This is a difficult task, as we might not find customary cues in people's body language in other cultures and may not be able to gauge what is going on. The first step toward understanding another culture is becoming aware of one's own cultural habits and values so that they will not interfere with learning those of the new culture. So, in trying to develop this tolerance threshold, it is important that we ourselves as teachers realize what our gut reactions to certain events are like and that we share these with our students transparently. As we share our own feelings and views, we also teach our students how to share theirs. In turn, the transparent sharing opens up a forum for discussion in a safe, non-judgmental environment where students and teachers alike can express their views freely. I often suggest a *Town Meeting* atmosphere for these discussions. Turn-taking, quality of individual participation, and organized personal presentations enrich these open discussions and allow those who would rarely speak out open up and do so in freedom. I recommend educators and school administrators to value the importance of this open line of communication so that we can better explore tolerance construction in schools.

ON THE CONCEPT OF CULTURE

Culture is the sum total of ways of living, including values, beliefs, aesthetic standards, linguistic expression, patterns of thinking, behavioral norms, and styles of communication which a group of people has developed to assure its survival in a particular physical and human environment. Culture and the people who are part of it interact so that culture is not static. Culture is the response of a group of human beings to the valid and particular needs of its members. It, therefore, has an inherent logic and an essential balance between positive and negative dimensions.

Most of culture lies hidden and is outside voluntary control. Even when small fragments of culture are elevated to awareness, they are difficult to change, not only because they are so personally experienced yet because people cannot act or interact at all in any meaningful way except through the medium of culture.

Helpful techniques for developing cross-cultural listening skills for example, require that you don't just listen to something, instead you are encouraged to listen for something. Listening to silence or for non-verbal cues or variations in voice intonation provide something to listen for. Learning how to ask questions or what questions to ask are also important cross-cultural considerations.

As we gain a cross-cultural perspective, we are harboring an alert, acute sense of awareness that we probably had not developed in the past. We are also learning how to rationalize about events differently. As we do this, we should be able to share our findings in a safe, non-judgmental environment so that we are free to grow in our newfound cross-cultural awareness.

PRACTICE EXERCISE

_____

_____

_____

_____

_____

REFLECTION EXERCISE

_____

_____

_____

_____

_____

Chapter Eleven

The Life-long Learner

Chapter eleven explores the concept of *life-long learner*, providing participants with information and tools for engaging in extended learning. Cultural icons, elements of popular culture that shape our thinking and contemporary issues are related to the goals of multicultural education. Readers explore popular culture and its effects on teaching and learning.

I would like to begin by sharing excerpts of an article I co-wrote with a colleague on the kinds of resistance we experienced while co-teaching a multicultural course (Asimeng-Boahene & Klein, 2004).

The growing cultural diversity of the United States makes it important to understand the importance of diverging values, customs, and traditions for multicultural learners. The minority thought or view may be just as equally legitimate and valid as the mainstream.

The *melting pot metaphor* does not apply any longer because it no longer describes the reality of the country accurately. Rather than a melting pot, we now have a tossed salad in which every segment maintains its own character.

However, because issues concerning diversity are delicate and complex. Diversity, however, pervades and persists no matter what the consequences are. The problems and challenges that educators encounter daily are many. These include lack of genuine educational and societal support, lack of teacher knowledge, parental disapproval, and lack of updated instructional materials.

The people who immigrate to the U.S are increasingly reluctant to forsake their cultural traditions and values to become like mainstream society. For instance, African Americans have fought or continue to fight to overcome oppression and discrimination so as to maintain their cultural heritage. Asians and Hispanics, also are often not overly excited in trading their ethnic customs and traditions in favor of European American habits (Manning &

Baruth, 2002). We are told by familiar demographic statistics that approximately, 33 percent of the American population growth during the 1980's was from immigration. This formed a 20 percent increase over the immigration rates that had existed since the 1940's. The 1990's have witnessed an increased influx of immigration from many countries. By the year 2000, demographers appraise that the United States will be only 72 percent European American, almost 13 percent African American, and 11 percent persons of Hispanic origin. Asian Americans and Native Americans will make up the remaining 4 percent. At present, students of color are the majority in twenty-five of the nation's largest school systems. One instructor commented on the lack of updated instructional resources and the lack of support for implementation of a multicultural agenda. This only happened when the entire educational unit came under accreditation review.

Traditionally, the curriculum has emphasized the acquisition of mainstream thought, not a multicultural way of knowing, let alone raising multicultural awareness. School administrators exert control over curricular content making little provision for diversity issues. They place more value on how students will test at the end of the year and how their school district will perform in front of taxpayers.

Teachers seldom include multicultural content in their daily instruction. Since teacher-education programs must eventually comply with the *Goals 2000* educational standards and the *No Child Left Behind Act* they are now being held accountable for covering the different educational curricula fully and for incorporating issues of diversity in their teaching.

This means that the integration of a multicultural perspective in teaching and learning is a widespread need. Accredited teacher-education programs must cover issues of diversity, multicultural awareness and sensitivity training towards implementing tolerance and acceptance in the curriculum.

However, there is a paradigm shift in teaching topics about multicultural education (Ukpokodu, 1999). We are more interested in promoting a global perspective. Hence, talking about how the "melting-pot" or "tossed salad" in America is no longer important. It is far more important to explore where our immigrants, refugees, migrant workers, and settlers came from. Teacher-candidates wishing to teach in elementary, middle school and high school are required to use real sources and to promote document-based questions in their future classrooms. The mandate we are hearing from research in curriculum & instruction is to promote the need for better and more equitable instructional teaching and for using authentic resources. We are also asking teacher candidates to explore, adopt, and understand (1) the Anti-bias curriculum (2) equitable educational teaching practices and (3) caring, student-centered teaching approaches.

Teaching programs for teacher candidates all over the United States now need to fulfill the cultural and linguistic diversity requirement to earn teaching credentials. So, as teacher-educators, we have many questions, inhibitions and intercultural clashes of our own.

Teaching equitably and teaching about equity in all classrooms is perhaps a more important issue than celebrating cultural congruence (Banks, 2000). The area of cultural and linguistic awareness is opening new avenues for class discussions in today's college classrooms. Bullying, harassment and stalking come up as salient school-related topics of discussion

Teaching about multicultural/global issues is difficult. Teacher-educators in general reflected on the need for collaboration, dialogue, and problem solving, to strengthen the field. An enlightening note, however, and quite revitalizing one indeed, is the finding that taking social action (Ooka Pang, 2002) becoming closely involved with colleagues in the field will strengthen all of us. The diversity issue is in fact a non-issue in some academic environments where there is little diversity among student and academic populations. Many campuses are addressing this situation by increasing diversity, attracting underrepresented minority students, and promoting multicultural awareness. These are healthy measures that will increase diversity in the long run, and will result in positive changes.

Teacher candidates should focus on developing critical awareness. Teacher educators must open the eyes of their students so that they are not consumers of instruction but actively engaged members of a global community. Teacher candidates should study the real issues that affect the world at large instead of developing a convenient post-card version of the world. The critically aware teacher candidate should also be encouraged to take a stance in life and to make decisions that promote a social conscience. How often do teachers turn a blind eye to the unfairness of the educational system, to the gravity of an issue that occurred on the playground, or to the discrepancies of their instruction *vis a vis* the curriculum.

As we empower our learners and raise the bar for our students to reach their potential through equitable learning processes, shouldn't teacher candidates be learning to model these desirable behaviors?

If teachers continue to feel disenfranchised by the system, if they live in fear and do not take social action because it may cause them their jobs, aren't we having them send a double message to their own students?

In conclusion, the above are some suggestions that can be implemented. Teacher educators need to (1) work from a sound conceptual framework (2) base their actions on theory research (3) act on issues instead of talking about them and (4) model an empowered, socially and critically aware instructor.

PRACTICE EXERCISE

REFLECTION EXERCISE

A Shared Dialogue

Chapter twelve is a shared dialogue with a multicultural educator/colleague and I. The dialogue shares how he is developing a multicultural perspective in his science classroom. Dr. Michael Jabot, a physics professor at SUNY Fredonia recounts how he is developing a course on multicultural science instruction for secondary school educators. From our conversations, I gather that he too is encountering the kinds of resistance I encountered in the past. We both teach in a rural area where communities have thrived together for generations with little or no diversity or variation. Immigration and mobility do not necessarily affect this community because during peek harvest season, migrant workers are hired to assist in these farming jobs.

The temporary workers that visit our area are housed, transported, and employed directly at the job-site. They rarely visit the area churches, parks and amenities. Their small children attend local daycare facilities set up for them. They also do minor grocery shopping in area convenient stores and food markets. Yet, based on my own interaction with them and from observing them carefully, they do not fully participate in the local community life.

Another interesting population we both work with is a transient group of families that come and go from Puerto Rico. The children who attend local schools where we place our students are either staying with relatives during the academic year, or residing in the area until they complete school. This community is more permanent than the migrating farmers, yet they too share very little with the local established rural community on a daily basis. They tend to reside in the same neighborhoods and participate in their own neighborhood activities. Some of their shops and entrepreneurial endeavors serve their own community, keeping a distance from the local rural community. The families children, and youth from this transient Puerto Rican community are embraced by both church and academic communities of the area. Families are accepted and integrated into the neighborhood schools as much as possible. What is most remarkable, however, is that the children themselves are the best equalizers. They play with, and include Puerto Rican children and youth in their everyday lives.

The college that we work at, however, is still working at expanding its cultural and ethnic diversity. Most of our students reflect the rural area that we are in. With rare exceptions there will probably be no racial or ethnic diversity in most of the courses that we teach. This makes it harder for us to talk about cultural awareness and tolerance-building that we attempt to do if we have such few members of the African American, Native American and Latino populations of students in our classrooms.

Aside from the cultural integration and demure cultural diversity issues we deal with in the classroom and outside, we both find that the curriculum has not varied much or adapted at all to the requirements and goals of a multicultural educational mind-set. Some schools demonstrate outward signs of interest in multicultural issues as they deck their walls with commemorative *realia* during Thanksgiving or Black History Month. Many schools own posters that they display for *Cinco de Mayo* celebrations thinking that all of their Latin American constituents celebrate this Mexican holiday.

What we find most difficult to do as instructors is to instill in our learners the importance of opening our minds and our hearts to the diverse ways of knowing. With this particular thought in mind, I like to spring forward as the Latina that I am and to explain that not all mathematics and science thinking is the same worldwide. Different cultures and different people share different views on how they process mathematics and science. We tend to believe that the entire world circles around our way of doing things. I emulate the great scientists and thinkers of past and present who do not reflect the Anglocentric/Eurocentric form of doing science and highlight the progress made by people from other cultures and other parts of the world. This effort to instill an understanding of multiple approaches to problem solving and to scientific methods makes my classroom explorations at the college vivid forums for comparison. I urge future science and mathematics educators

As I started to think about what it was going to mean for a physicist to start to teach a course on multi-cultural education, it came to mind, that I should start to follow some of the advice that James Banks gives us. This means to think about our lives through a multicultural perspective and to sort-out elements from our cultural autobiography. I grew up in very suburban, Upstate New York town. My Mom and Dad were from the era that if you graduated from High School, you went straight to work. So I was the first in my family to go onto college. My Dad quit high school to enter the Navy at the end of World War II. Went back to high school and finished and then was drafted back into the Korean Conflict. He worked as a fireman, a carpenter building our house and all the other houses in our neighborhood. Ended his work career running a construction company building roads and bridges, tracks and tennis courts. Probably my most persistent memory of my Dad growing up was my Dad leaving for work at 4:00 in the morning six days a week and coming home at 8:00 at night. I don't think I really understood what that meant for my sister and me. Both my mother, who has worked at the same job as a secretary for 52 years, and my father did everything that they could for my sister and I. Every penny that they made went into trying to make our lives the best they could be. I think like every kid, I don't know as if I appreciated that growing up. I know that I appreciate it much more today. My Dad was always concerned about how well I was doing in school. I guess at the time I just thought it was his being just a dad. He always shared his view that if someone got ahead of you in life because they were smarter than you. That was one thing. But if they got ahead of you in life because they worked harder than you than that was your fault. And he never wanted to see me outworked by anybody..I was never allowed to have a job growing up, because school was my job. My summer job was always running a jackhammer, or finishing concrete. Always a job that would make me realize, that studying hard was easier than working this hard. He wanted me to be so tired at the end of the day that I was too tired to spend the money the made over the summer so it would all go into the college account. Looking back at it now, he realized that if I was going to go further than he did I need to do well in school and go on to college. I think that it meant more to my Dad when I graduated from college than it did to me. He realized that my college degree meant something in society and that having it opened doors for me that were never open to him. I graduated from high school and seemed to have lots of friends and all my friends seemed to look a lot like me We had very few students of color in our school. We grew up in an area that had a very large native population, but those students were never in class with us. We had one African-American family in town and we all looked at them as being the same as us. I don't think that I ever realized that weren't just like us, until my junior year when Bob asked Jessie to go to the Prom with him. The uproar that that caused made me realize that Jessie and her family were seen as being very different than the rest of us. My only other memory of interacting with people of color came through the people that worked for my Dad's construction company. My Dad asked the paving crew to come to our house after work. What left the greatest impression was that not all of the guys on the crew would come into our house. Nate, the hardest working most talented guy on the whole crew, was a man of color. When he came to our house, Nate wouldn't even come into our house. Instead he sat on a bucket in the driveway until everyone was done and ready to leave. Because he was black, he had learned that you didn't go into our house. I remember that same guy who sat in our driveway calling my Dad at 3:00 in the morning and my Dad waking me up to go with him to pick him up after he had been arrested for DWI. My Dad was the only person that he felt he could call. So we drove the 25 miles to pick him up, bail him out and took him home. I also remember going with my Dad to Nate's funeral. We were the only the white people in the whole funeral home. As strange as Nate must have felt in coming into our "world", I felt stranger at his funeral. I made to point of saying that no one in our town looked very different from anyone else, because I really do think that that was the attitude we took, as naive as it was, that we were all the same. It was quite a shock when I went away to college to find out that not everybody saw people in the same way that my friends and I growing up had. It was in seeing the distrust that others had based on their life experience really did change the way that I looked at many of the issues in my life especially in my years of teaching. After I graduated from college I came back to the same town I grew up in and began to teach in the high school there. I taught physics and science for 15 years. I think that when I stared teaching I had the same attitude toward school and the kids in the school as I did growing up. I think a lot of us considered most of the kids to be the same. I think that that is when I started to realize the population I had grown-up with was really very different than how I perceived it and more importantly how I was perceived by those same kids I grew up with. Looking back on the town I grew up in, I realize how divided the community really was amongst class. The town is very much a bedroom community for two larger cities and very much filled with doctors and lawyers and other professional people, which our family wasn't. I think my parents spent our whole lives growing up trying to be sure that we didn't look different than the kids in the town. For the most part I think everyone described our house the same way they described everyone else's house, but for very different reasons. I think everyone of my friends thought my Dad was an engineer. He wasn't an engineer he had a high school diploma. But I think whet he and my Mom did was to make sure that we "looked" the same as the other kids in town so we wouldn't stand out. As I started to teach in the town, I started to realize that not all of the kids looked the same. That for the most part our community had many, many people that lived very close to the poverty line. We had a lot of people that were farmers and pickers on the onion and potato farms and lived very much hand to mouth. They probably did not have any of the things that my sister and I had growing up and that we didn't appreciate. I think the turning point in my career in terms of being sensitive to issues of diversity, was having one of my teaching colleagues describe his idea that the "world needs ditch-diggers". What this person meant by this was that we needed to have an educational program that was stratified just like our society is stratified. That we needed to have an educational system for those doctors' and lawyers' kids who were going to be professionals and a different and not equal system for those kids that came from those poor homes. My most shocking realization was that when this person described ditch diggers he was literally talking about my Dad. In turn he was describing the system of education that I should have received and would not have allowed me to go onto college as I had. This person was one of my teachers as I went through school. I am convinced that based on how I looked, on the friends I had, on looking at the house I lived in, he never realized the reality that my father did nothing but *work to be sure that we looked the same as everybody else. I think that at that point I decided that the world probably does need ditch diggers and that we needed to do the best that we can to help those kids. This is not accomplished by supporting a stratified system. Children shouldn't grow up having much less than the other kids do. I'd rather we created a system where our focus was on helping those students learn. For that reason I started to teach courses that nobody else wanted to teach because they did not want to teach THOSE kids. I started to teach applied physics to kids who would tear their cars apart and learn physics that way. I think it was then that I realized that most of the kids in my neighborhood growing up thought that I had a different bike every week because I would take my father's tools in the garage and take my whole bike apart. Then I would put it back together again with any remaining parts going into a coffee can and start over the next week. I think that I was a lot more like THOSE kids I was teaching in the applied physics class that I was teaching than I was like my friends growing up. It was also in working with the students in the applied physics course that I realized what teaching actually was. I was blessed with a skill set that allowed me to make sense of even bad teaching in math and science. The students in the applied classes did not have this skill set and were not polite enough to tell me that I was doing a good job when I wasn't. They would call me out and tell me that I needed to a better job in explaining what I was asking of them. In needing to do a better job explaining, I needed to understand the content I was teaching much better. In understanding my content better and understanding better what it meant to teach I also started to realize the important role that I as a teacher played in my students' lives. I don't know how many times I stood in my house and would hear a roar from a car coming down the street. Looking out the window, one of my students would be pulling into the driveway to show me the car that they had fixed up. I recall the times when miraculous things would happen. For example, a lawn mower showing up at my house after mentioning that mine was broken, only to have to go back into the class and say; "Thanks to who ever brought the mower to my house yesterday, but please return it to where ever you borrowed it from." It was the first time that these students had ever been treated in the way we wanted to be treated. Once I took the time and opportunity to treat them with a level of respect for the special talents that each of them had they would run through a burning building for me. My greatest achievements in teaching had nothing to do with a perfect Regents passing record that I had in every year I taught Physics or in the number of students who got great scores in the Advanced Placement Physics. My greatest success stories were those applied physics students who went on from my class to outperform students who were coming from a place of privilege, just because they were given a chance. Poverty in our town was generational and I don't think that any of the students in my courses had aspirations beyond what their parents had obtained and certainly not that of going on to college. What I hoped I did in my class was to allow the students to see that the individual gifts that each of them brought were important. Whether it is knowing how to solve a differential equation or knowing how to machine a part both of these play an important role in our society. The successes of my teaching had little to do with students who achieved high scores on tests in spite of my bad teaching. The successes that I had in class were in helping students who needed me to be at the top of my profession in order for them to do well. And having them do well is a much more valid measure of success than scores on a standardized test. The moral of my story has a couple of important points. First is that for most of my professional life I missed the opportunity to take advantage of what students have to offer. This is ultimately the goal of multicultural education. To start where the students are; to understand that each of us has a story to tell; each of us have gifts that we bring to the classrooms and that we as teachers need to take advantage of those gifts at every opportunity. I think I had always defined multiculturalism as speaking a different language. But now I think that multiculturalism is just that each of us brings our own "culture" to the classroom and that our culture colors how we see the world around us and certainly "colors" how we hear what a teacher tries to help us understand. I hope that I can help future math and science teachers avoid the mistakes that I have made. The second point is that we need to understand our own lives in a way that will allow us to be honest with our students. Part of being honest is to allow our students to see who we are, the chinks in our armor, the good the bad and the indifferent. For the first part of my teaching career I pretended to be someone I wasn't not because I wanted to be dishonest, I just didn't know enough about who I really was to be honest with students. Our responsibility as professionals is to help ALL students achieve. Whether a student is going onto an Ivy League school or is one of THOSE kids, we have the professional and moral responsibility to help them achieve. As a physics teacher and more particu-*

larly a teacher of science, I need to address multicultural issues in a way that provides a theoretical framework for exploring and developing a culturally responsive approach to the teaching of science. In exploring instructional formats that incorporate a global approach to teaching and learning, I hope to help the candidates' in my courses to develop approaches that prepare them for an ever-increasing population of students that reflect diverse backgrounds and abilities. This is done best by allowing the students to share their own experiences in learning as I have in this critical reflection.

PRACTICE EXERCISE

REFLECTION EXERCISE

Chapter Thirteen

Multiculturalizing Thematic Units

Chapter thirteen offers a blueprint for well-designed thematic units. Several units are critiqued and improved. Ways of multiculturalizing instruction are shared. Readers multiculturalize teaching ideas.

THEORIES ON MULTICULTURALIZING
INSTRUCTIONAL MATERIALS

At this point in time, I'd like to present an idea that I have borrowed from textbook authors Davidman & Davidman, and Cushner. This idea evolves from the concept of instructional planning using a multicultural perspective, or what they've coined to be *multiculturalizing* instructional plans.

All three authors devote extensive portions of their books to instructional design. The basic premise for this design lies in using a multicultural lens or focus to develop instruction around equitable teaching practices and diversity awareness. In order to make this happen in today's classrooms, we need to in our instructional motivation and to understand what we teach with informed choices and knowledge bases. Hence, as we prepare our instructional units, teachers should become more knowledgeable about the topics they are teaching and they should teach for more lasting learning.

James Banks urges us to move away from the celebrations approach, which he so much objects to and to think of a multi-pronged approach to instruction. He says that teachers and educational systems have perpetuated the use of a handed-down instructional platform based on a few misconceptions about the world, a little storytelling about world-events and lots of surface teaching. He describes what he denominates the *celebrations approach*. This is where we pick and choose international topics for their entertainment value. Hence, as

I've said repeatedly within this book, and I include myself in this accusation, we teach to topics of interest that we can embellish in the classroom so as to develop a travelogue-approach of the world with our students.

Rather than just teaching about Egypt; just because we can conveniently snap in and out of two historical eras and learn about pictographic writing, we shouldn't be teaching about Mexico just because it borders the United States. We should instead teach what we can connect to our daily lives. Hence we teach topics where students and teachers engage in dialogue, ask good questions, connect ideas and relate what they are learning to a broader context. As we carry out the *multiculturalization* exercises, let's keep these in mind.

Historically, when multicultural ideas have been shared in the classroom, they center around celebratory dates or seasonal time-frames. Somehow, teachers incorporate the idea in their classroom that we live in a global world by introducing the foods, folklore, and traditions of a particular country to drive this point across. If we learn how to *multiculturalize* a lesson properly, we won't have to delay our teaching and wait for the holiday or season to happen so that we can teach about it.

Let's talk about the three-pronged approach. I'm sure lots of you have taught in this way or have experienced it in your previous learning. Have you ever stopped to ask yourselves while teaching about the American Revolution, what the Frenchman or the Native American felt at the time? Have you ever been interested in finding out what British Loyalists felt about this scenario?

Or, were you like myself drawn by the events of the Boston Tea Party or the issues of Taxation without Representation? My fourth grade teacher was very excited about these events in history. She shared captions from old newspapers, showed us pictures and illustrations about the political upheaval and explained the newfound nationalism in the Thirteen Colonies with a passion. She narrated these as stories with vivid detail for our delight. Back then, we didn't have the *Internet* or the *Discovery Channel* or *PBS*. The only textbook that we had, did not use a three-pronged approach or any critical thinking format for us to analyze what we were reading. Basically, like many North American textbooks produced in the 1950's, it covered the events and issues from a nationalistic point of view. We were taught history by being told about events, never sharing what could have happened or what else was happening in the rest of the world. I distinctly remember this to be true throughout my entire elementary-school education. Today, fortunately, our students are being taught by authentic documents and realistic learning formats so that they can learn within a context and so that they can think for themselves.

James Loewen, in his book *Lies My Teacher Told Me* has explored this one-sided, often misrepresented point of view in great depth. He has carefully scrutinized history textbooks written for our generations of students and has corroborated this one-dimensional story line. The Internet and the wide avail-ability of primary sources now allow us to explore, question and uncover other truths. Other authors have joined Loewen in this deep quest for truth, and teachers are now empowered to join as well.

Give your students the opportunity to discover and uncover history for themselves. Create learning situations where they can dig for artifacts, just like the anthropologist does. Channel their curiosity by providing them with the instruments they need to probe for evidence like detectives do.

Popular culture today is permeated with models that you can use to moti-vate your students to become explorers. Don the science fiction mask or the CSI magnifying glass or the Indiana Jones hat as you talk about the ways these specialists find evidence and unearth the truth. The following are a few helpful exercises for you to look into as you multiculturalize your instruc-tional units.

In the textbook *Teaching with a Multicultural Perspective* (2001), the au-thors, Davidman & Davidman devote an entire section of the book to ex-plaining how to add, retrieve and include information that makes instructional units multiculturally designed. They spend time taking apart elementary and secondary school instructional units that would otherwise have been fine, hadn't we acquired this new lens and instructional perspective. Let me walk you through some of these.

On page 170, they walk you through some popular instructional activities now enhanced through their multicultural lens. They begin by critiquing a program called the *word of the week*. Through this critique they contest that although the program has good intentions, it lacks a focus on parental in-volvement and does little to promote cultural pluralism, inter-group harmony, and equitable treatment of all students. The reasons for this are that the pro-gram only rewards one or two students from each class per week as they se-lect recipients of the award. The word selection and the reward system be-come an almost elitist idea, which strays from the original intention of the program. Davidman & Davidman recommend that to make this program more multiculturally-sensitive (1) representatives from the parent committee be included in the word selection (2) recipients of the weekly award be con-sidered representatives of an entire student body as opposed to winners of the award (3) recipients sharing the prize equitably.

Next, they critique a current events program, designed around the social studies curriculum. Originally, the program involves students sharing their media findings. In this current events program, students bring an article they've found to class. They can also report on a newscast they have listened to. The basic idea behind doing this is to instill in young learners a habit of reading newspapers and listening to broadcast news. Davidman & Davidman, suggest that the classroom teacher involve parents in this process more. They also include the idea of linking media awareness to something more tangible and lasting like creating a classroom library containing documents that support each process that is explored. Finally, they suggest some type of follow-through where the event, activity or process becomes channeled into something that is in continual change and evolution.

Finally, they critique an all-time favorite teacher-activity, oral reading. This is still a classic teaching activity that involves the teacher reading from important pieces of literature to students. Davidman & Davidman don't object to this type of teacher-directed learning. They suggest that we continue using this learning format, however with a few modifications, such as, selecting a theme or topic that can be extended, and relating the oral reading to a subsequent activity that students carry out on their own. Again, we want to remind you that self-regulation continues to be important. So, as we read aloud to our students, we need to be vigilant so that our students don't turn off and pretend they are listening to us. We want to channel their academically-engaged minds into doing something productive after the shared reading. Other recommendations are that the teacher finds ways to really involve the listeners so that they too participate in this invaluable activity.

In section two of their book, Davidman & Davidman describe ways to multiculturalize lesson plans and thematic units. I'd recommend that you get a hold of this invaluable book and flip through these pages on your own, as I don't want to summarize their book for you. However, I find it useful, as I flip through these suggestions, to see that everything I've already told you is still good teaching and makes good common sense. So, while planning classroom activities the rules of thumb for cooperative team-work are:

1. Try to use four-member cooperative learning teams (as I've already told you, sometimes a three-member team can be unproductive)
2. Provide all team-members with enough information about what they are expected to do
3. Reinforce team-members for what they are doing well.

Again I've mentioned these to you before, remember what we said about the engaged, self-regulated, motivated student who knows just precisely where, what, when, and how the task will be done. This is a student who needs your constant support and reinforcement, as well as clear and direct guidelines. But it's all about his/her own learning and sense of agency. We supply them with the tools and resources to allow them to manufacture a product, which results in their own learning.

Chapter Thirteen

PRACTICE EXERCISE

REFLECTION EXERCISE

Chapter Fourteen

Curricular Constraints & Challenges

Chapter fourteen celebrates our progress and assists us in moving forward. We discuss *curricular constraints*, the effects of standardized testing agendas in our teaching, and the administrative hurdles we encounter as we continue on our teaching/learning journey. As the well-informed, socially aware change agents that we have become, we generate strategies for dealing with these issues multiculturally. Readers generate a school-wide multicultural reform agenda.

THEORIES ON CURRICULAR CONSTRAINTS

At this point in time, you will already have experienced the classroom, created innovative and exciting thematic units and lesson-plans. You probably feel very excited about your teaching career. I commend you on what you have accomplished and bless you with the power to continue doing what you do so well in your future classrooms. You will have recourse to many ideas and formats that you've collected throughout your study program. You will also have valuable insights from your mentor teachers and from your graduate studies programs.

I would like to share the results of some research I have been conducting with my colleague, Dr. Andrea Zevenbergen (Psychology Department, SUNY Fredonia) on the impact of standardized testing in schools.

In their longitudinal study on the effect of high-stakes testing on students, Madaus & Clarke (2001) conclude that *High-stakes, high-standards tests do not have a markedly positive effect on teaching and learning in the classroom and do not motivate the unmotivated.*

Data from research conducted at Boston College over 30 years highlight 4 issues: (1) High stakes, high standards tests do not have a markedly positive effect on teaching and learning. (2) High stakes tests do not motivate the unmotivated. (3) Authentic high stakes assessments are not a more equitable way to assess the progress of students who differ in race, culture, native language, or gender and (4) high stakes testing programs have been shown to increase high school dropout rates, particularly among minority populations.

Standardized and High Stakes tests measure public school districts' and campuses' performance (Kamii, 1989; Pedroza,1998; Popham, 1987). The results of these tests are publicly shared with districts, communities and stakeholders affecting not only student performance but that of schools, administrators, and teachers.

The history of standardized testing evolves after 1950 (Kamii, 1989) where accountability was measured by test results escalating the number of tests given to children exponentially. After the publication of A Nation at Risk (National Commission on Excellence in Education, 1983) more testing was implemented in schools to measure outcomes. President Bush's Bill No Child Left Behind (2000) sanctions schools who do not perform well on standardized tests. The pressure is on for better results and outcomes.

The literature on standardized testing discusses in general that minority populations of people experience alienation, disenfranchisement and *marginalization* in many public schools. This is true particularly in schools that are administered by individuals of majority culture. Standardized testing may be another venue within which this alienation occurs, and it may exacerbate separation between people of minority culture and school systems.

Pedroza (1998), in a study conducted in the state of Texas, found that language-minorities and economically disadvantaged student populations were identified as low-performing schools. Details from this data inform readers that in 1993, 90% of the students in 333 individual schools identified in the state of Texas, students who performed worse were African American or Hispanic

Insights gleaned from educators and test-designers (Kamii, 1989; Popham, 2001; Protheroe, 2001) draw our attention to conceptual and linguistic misconceptions experienced by both African American and Hispanic students who (1) do not speak standard English at home and (2) do not have sufficient exposure to standard English. They also point out that SES affects exposure to the types of information that might appear on tests. For example, students of low SES do not have access to media or print media that would otherwise inform them of geographic, scientific and social information often present in tests.

James Popham details such conceptual and linguistic misconceptions where the test questions address issues that students haven't been taught or exposed to. In some cases, the test questions are not only poorly designed but grammatically incorrect. To cite a Fifth Grade Language Arts item:

Our music teacher was surprised when *Jill and me sang* the wrong note. Which are the correct words for this sentence?

1. *Jill and me sung*
2. *Jill and I will sing*
3. *Jill and I sang*
4. *No mistake*

He questions the use or misuse of I and me as a problem already, taking away the focus from the verb to sing. The student taking this test is unsure of which one of the two errors to address. I personally have problems with incorrect punctuation on this test item, requiring a period at the end of all of the sentences presented above.

Another example from a Fourth Grade Reading Item:

My father's *field* is computer graphics.

In which of the sentences below does the word *field* mean the same thing as in the sentence above?

1. *The shortstop knew how to field his position.*
2. *We prepared the field for plowing it.*
3. *What field do you plan to enter when you graduate?*
4. *The nurse examined my field of vision.*

The commentary here is that the concept of field in this situation is very sophisticated. Most children understand job or employment as opposed to field of expertise. If a child taking this test has parents who do not have a specific field of expertise, for example, this question would be over their heads, as per house cleaning or window cleaning, which are not fields of expertise.

The faults in design of tests are one of the many problems reported in the literature. Other problems that surface are those where testing and teaching to the test detract from other types of learning that occur in the classroom. Questions as to whether high stakes standardized tests truly reflect a learner's potential and capabilities and their progress arise (Madaus, & Clarke (2001); Morris (2000). Progress and academic growth are not only reflected in this type of assessment (Richman, 2001) because the type of accountability addressed in the test results reflect the progress of an entire school community that is under federal support or under scrutiny for obtaining federal support.

A review of the literature on a more positive impact of standardized testing points to the fact that (Levinson, 2000) in many countries progress and academic growth are aligned with standard forms of assessment. What happens in these countries (England, Canada, Japan, Australia and the Czech Republic) is that both the curriculum and the tests are created and developed by the same educational agencies. The test itself is seen as a mechanism for promoting the curriculum. The common element in the testing produced in the aforementioned countries is that of raising the bar and elevating standards.

Hence, the curriculum and the quality of instruction are aligned with the expectations within the test. The interesting result here is the match between higher results and higher quality instruction. Madaus & Clarke (2001) find that standardized high stakes testing do not have a positive effect on teaching and learning, and do not motivate the unmotivated. However, interestingly enough, as Popham (2002) reports, the 1970's and 1980's promoted a minimum competency format in the tests. Well-designed tests that are aligned with high standards that are clearly specified and represented in the curriculum are positive key factors. So, and in good measure, a strong curriculum that is shaped by the needs measured in the test, paired with good teaching is not a bad combination.

For clarification purposes, our state places heavy importance on Board of Regents Examinations. The results of these examinations define whether high school students are ready for college or not. The Regents Examinations along with (AP) Advanced Placement courses taken in high school enable high school students to be exempt from some college courses as freshmen and sophomores in college.

Without a strong (ESL) English as a Second Language program, and with very few trained professionals in ESL instruction issues are dealt with as: (1) resource room pullout or, (2) a discipline problem (one participant mentioned the fact that the language barrier usually results in the child being labeled ADD).

Funding for special programs is based on eligibility and test results. In many cases the existing indicators provide continuity in funding, so there's a let it be treatment of the lack of ESL support for students.

Another reality is that youngsters do not maintain a constant schedule of attendance. Extended absences due to their family situation might cause a youngster to be away from school for a long period of time, resulting in lots of lessons missed. Another, culturally based situation is that the language spoken at home is not a dialogic, where the youngsters carry out a conversation with their caregivers. Latin American parenting formats, for example, do not usually encourage open conversations or much dialogue. Children are seen but not heard. Parents are also not always present throughout the school day or when youngsters return from school as they might be working the evening shift or two shifts in all.

Research indicates that the *Latino Ways of Knowing* are reflected by the way the family interacts together and the treatment of children by adults. Respect is the attitude that holds the fabric of Hispanic/Latino society together. A young child is not going to interact with a North-American teacher that is not of Hispanic origin in the same way as he/she will act towards relatives and peers. History tells us that Hispanics settled a great part of the North American territory (California, Arizona, New Mexico, Texas and Colorado). Education then was imparted through Roman Catholic parochial schools. In the family unit, Latino families are typically child-centered, young children are given the most attention. They are taught at home that it is disrespectful to look a person of authority in the eye, especially when being reprimanded. Instead, they demonstrate respect by looking down and away from the direct stare of the adult.

This might bring up a series of problems in a classroom situation unless the teacher knows about this cultural aspect. Abi-Nader (in Nieto, p. 147) describes a project carried out amongst Latino youth in the Northeast. In this classroom interactions between the teacher and students are based on Latino cultural values of *familia* A sense of caring and support is transmitted. The teacher becomes like a father, brother and friend to students. He also has high expectations for them and teaches them to take collective responsibility for one another through activities such as peer tutoring and mentoring. The focus is on extending the family. This would be ideal in the learning situations in schools in Town D. Some classrooms are very inviting of the Latino population, especially in the schools that have the larger Puerto Rican/Mexican cohorts. However, the problem lies in the history of the area, where much resentment towards this community arose back in the sixties. Many of the teachers in the area were not used to teaching such diverse classrooms and the quick rate of growth in the Latino cohort has forced them to modify their educational goals. There's a feeling of having to slow down.

According to Nieto (p. 146) recent research in the pedagogy of African American teachers of African American students shows teachers using their cultural knowledge and experiences to overcome the many negative messages students have been receiving. They use their students' culture to bridge the gap. They use empowering pedagogy encouraging students to think critically and to work actively for social justice.

From this overview of the impact of our research questions and the response from our participants, we can gather that there is a definite problem related to testing in the area. As one participant relays the anxiety her own young ones feel, another participant corroborates the labeling issue as her child was held back due to bad test results, labeling of students surfaces as a constant problem. Our data is clearly indicating that: (1) We need to listen to the needs of our community (2) Our community needs to let administrators, staff and boards know what their needs are by becoming involved. (3) We need to customize instruction to the needs of our community. (4) We need to remove anxiety from the testing situation as it will be no longer an issue if left alone.

It also reveals, consistently, that some community members feel alienated by their school system. Their children aren't being offered a fair chance in life as they are labeled as failure before they have an opportunity to grow as people. Their concerns are not voiced as their ways of knowing and learning aren't represented in the way teaching and learning is managed.

Some communities have more inter-communal support through their church organizations and from stakeholders who represent its members. There is a high level of marginalization as a result of not feeling their concerns matter. There is also a high expectation for *transiency* from the school administrators and teachers, as if because of the nature of the Puerto Rican life-style and the migrant worker's situation, presence along a continuum determines how poorly they will do on standardized tests. Some communities rely on strong leadership while others are totally disenfranchised and misrepresented. There is language and life-style difference that is characteristic in the Latino population in particular, as although the Spanish language is a commonality, not all Mexican and Puerto Rican Latinos speak Castillian Spanish correctly and perhaps were not schooled at all prior to arriving to Town D.

PRACTICE EXERCISE

_____

_____

_____

_____

_____

REFLECTION EXERCISE

_____

_____

_____

_____

_____

Chapter Fifteen

Charting our Own Journey

Chapter fifteen culminates our journey by celebrating our transformation and empowering us to continue doing what we already do so well. Readers reflect back and put closure on the issues that arose during their visceral self-disclosure exercises done in the first chapters. They generate their own *Magna Carta* or *Bill of Rights* for multicultural education to flourish in their classrooms. They reflect on the challenges they will face in their future endeavors.

THEORIES ON YOUR TEACHING JOURNEY

You are now ready to embark on your own teaching journey. You've completed the toolkit consisting of self-disclosure exercises, cultural awareness-building, designing multiculturized instructional materials, procuring context-rich teaching formats for your students, promoting self-regulated learning, using adequate classroom management and instructional tools, and above all, a gleaning a self-actualized awareness which translates into a way of knowing that is empowering. You "can do anything" from now on.

You're probably equipped with a running portfolio of things you've created. These include letters of recommendation from host teachers, professors and administrators that you've worked with. You are full of ideas and raring to go. You're probably wondering what this chapter is all about and whether it's worth your while, since you've already "done everything you had to do".

However, let me tell you, this chapter and its reflective exercises are perhaps the most important of all. You're aware of the conceptual framework that we embrace here at SUNY Fredonia. We use the *PIRR model* (planning, instruction, reflecting, and responding) to carry out the many tasks we do both in the college classroom and in schools. This last chapter requires that you respond and apply all of the above candid and openly.

In terms of planning, what will you be doing in your classroom? How will you plan your instruction to suit the needs of your students? How will you include all of the things you've learned as well as keep up with the demands and constraints of our standards-based, highly tested teaching and learning environment? Let me give you a brief heads up on what's happening in school districts nation-wide. Here's a summary of a research study Dr. Zevenbergen and I conducted on the impact of standardized testing in schools and how teachers cope with this reality.

Educational accountability is incrementally measured through standardized testing in U.S. schools and school districts. Student demographics are changing quickly and underrepresented youth and their families are often excluded or alienated by this process. A concerned team of researchers, namely a clinical psychologist and a teacher-educator, set out to measure the impact of incremental standardized testing on their community. Surveys were delivered to 200 elementary, middle, and secondary-school-educators. 21 responses were analyzed using the Constant Comparative Method (Glaser & Strauss, 1967) within qualitative research inquiry (Lincoln & Guba, 1985; Maykut & Morehouse, 1994). Results from the study reveal that standardized testing affects the focus of instruction. Teachers prepare students year-round (they teach to the test.) Teachers also perform test-related, preparative instruction, which governs most of their curricula. On a more positive note, some teachers said that testing allows them to develop more focused teaching experiences for their students. Studies like these are important because classroom inquiry of this kind provides insights into the needs of practitioners in the field.

Standardized testing permeates school life from grade 2 to 11 in our district. The literature points out that parents, legislators, and constituents expect high achievement and accountability in education. In this day and age of a technological revolution there is a generalized need for keeping up with the rest of the world. The literature on improving education and raising the bar on expectations coincides with the goals set forth by standards-based instruction. Aligning standards to the curriculum has met with positive results. Parents, administrators and legislators at large want to hold schools accountable for the education of their constituents.

Teachers, however, have different views about standardized testing. They feel that in many cases, testing drives instruction and doesn't reflect what students know (Madaus & Clarke, 2000). The literature indicates that when teachers spend time preparing students for tests, they focus on tests and neglect their instructional plan (Lynd, 2000). Teachers also find that testing brings out the more competitive nature in their learners and that too much emphasis is placed on test performance rather than on long-term learning.

Interested in this phenomenon, we used a survey questionnaire with teachers in our district to find out how they cope and manage with standardized testing. We delivered 200 questionnaires to five schools (k–12) in Western New York. Of these five schools, 3 were elementary, 2 were middle schools and 1 was a high school. Twenty-two participants returned the questionnaires. However, one questionnaire included no responses and was not analyzed. Twenty participants provided information on gender; there were 20% males and 70% females. Of 19 participants providing information regarding what grade they taught, 43% taught elementary school, 29% taught middle school and 19% taught high school. The mean length of teaching was 15.0 years (SD = 12.24 years); twenty participants provided information on race. Of these 20, 78% were Caucasian.

We created the questionnaire to generally assess ways of managing standardized testing. The questionnaire also assessed teachers' thoughts regarding advantages and disadvantages of standardized testing in schools. There were eight questions, which basically addressed the following:

1. The impact of testing on teachers and students.
2. The way teachers manage instruction towards testing.
3. The way teachers handle student learning while testing.
4. Data was analyzed using the constant comparative method (Glaser & Strauss, 1967). This method of analyzing qualitative data combines inductive category coding with a simultaneous comparison of all units of meaning obtained. Using an inductive approach, we examined the meaning behind the participants' words on the questionnaires. We were interested in developing propositions: statements of fact inductively derived from a rigorous and systematic analysis of the data (Maykut & Morehouse, 1994). We identified small units of meaning, unitizing the data. We later created larger categories based on the common threads of meaning (Lincoln & Guba, 1985). We cut apart each questionnaire creating categories using common features in responses. As each new unit of meaning was selected for analysis, it was compared to all other units of meaning and categorized.

Results showed the following; of all the statements made regarding standardized testing, 77% were negative and 23% were positive. The data were divided into five main categories: (1) curriculum influence (2) influence on students: (3) accountability as predictor of school success (4) test content and (5) influence on students. Specific coping strategies managed by teachers reflect the fact that 33% prepare students for format and 71% teach test-content throughout the academic year. Further results showed that 24% used test-driven teaching, 58% generally taught test content and 4% provide authentic instruction. Looking at the teaching to the test data, one could say that 14% teach test-taking strategies, 33% focus on organization, 14% model evaluation and 33% prepare students mentally. With respect to other data 14% decrease other demands on students during testing season, 14% give accommodations where required, 23% encourage healthy behaviors and 19% offer an appropriate test environment.

Out of the 33% of respondents addressing the issue of preparing students for the test format, 100% shared comments on how they do parallel testing tasks in class. In anticipation of the tests, some of these tasks include (1) explaining test expectations to students (2) previewing the format of the tests (3) allowing early exposure through administering an old exam and (4) providing Board of Regents-style test questions regularly. Teacher comments included:

"I discuss the test with the students. We do several activities which mirror the test format, so the children aren't so intimidated by it."

"From September to January, we totally taught to the ELA test. We used practice books and parallel tasks to ready them for the test. Very little authentic reading took place."

In terms of authentic instruction, one teacher said she uses authentic literature to prepare students for the test. Another teacher integrates the individual learning styles of her students so that they all have opportunities to practice test taking in the way they learn best.

Organization, modeling, budgeting time, and encouraging healthy behaviors among students were also foci of attention for teachers. Year-round, they practiced these skills with students, encouraging them to plan ahead, to break down information into a manageable size, to read instructions clearly, and to stay focused. Three teachers, for example, modeled the way tests are scored for students to make them aware of what counts on the test. Three teachers also talked about reducing the level of stress in their classrooms by encouraging a calming attitude and promoting a positive learning environment.

They also mentioned keeping parents informed of the onset of testing season and reducing homework assignments during that time period. Emphasis was placed on nutrition, rest, and bringing comfortable clothing and a water bottle to school.

The results of our study indicate overall, that standardized testing does currently affect teaching and learning in our community. This is especially exacerbated because this is a pivotal year for the implementation of the English

Language Assessment (ELA) as well as the yearly discipline-specific tests that will be administered. Aside from the test-related constraints placed on school administrators and schoolteachers' high expectations for improvement influence the tone of teaching and learning as well as the school climate.

New legislation currently affecting all educational settings in the United States promotes a need for accountability and in incremental record of success in all public schools. Schools that fall behind are short-changing students who by law are entitled to equitable teaching and learning opportunities. In our view, and using the information gleaned from our data, all of these constraints put lots of pressure on school administrators and schoolteachers, because the evaluation process is so transparent. As more information is shared about how well or how badly school districts are performing more anxiety arises. All of these tensions create a testing agenda that is not always beneficial to young learners.

After summarizing our findings, we ponder whether authentic instructional formats (portfolio assessment, creative reading and writing opportunities, and lab-style math and science forums) are being lost. We also wonder whether teacher's strategies are likely to lead to higher scores on tests, in detriment of lasting knowledge-construction. Ultimately, as we continue to study this process, we would like to measure the kinds of teaching and learning that are, in fact, more lasting formats.

Don't think this is a silly question. The person I respected the most at my doctoral institution asked me this same question during my doctoral defense. I was quite surprised about this question. However, after thinking about it for a few minutes I realized how important it truly was. This question has shaped my career.

Let me explain why this question is so important. The professor who first asked me this is an ethnographer. Her job is to go into a place, environment, situation, and check it out. Like a detective, she enters a new environment breathing it all in, sorting things out and posing questions. She begins to gather information about the place, stacking and piling it into manageable mental binders, expecting to sort it all out at the end. Everything is important, as she scrutinizes an area, looking at the general and the specific in great detail. To find meaning around her, she first sorts out her first impressions. What are people doing? What are they saying to each other? What is important? What goes on indoors, outdoors, within hallways? Who is in control? How is this control handled and managed? What are the prospective conflicts? What creates conflict? What harmonizes the place? How does the environment affect the location? Is there noise and interference? How do people relate to this?

PRACTICE EXERCISE

REFLECTION EXERCISE

References

Allport, Gordon. (1954). *The nature of prejudice*. NY: Doubleday Anchor Books.

Armstrong, Thomas. (2000). *Multiple intelligences in the classroom*. (2nd Ed). Alexandria, VA: ASCD.

Banks, James A. (2003). *Teaching strategies for ethnic studies*. (seventh edition). NY: Allyn & Bacon.

————. (2001). *Cultural diversity and education*. Boston, MA: Allyn & Bacon.

Barba, Roberta H. (1998). *Science in the multicultural classroom*. Boston, MA: Allyn & Bacon.

Bogardus, Emory. (1940). *Social thought*. NY: Longmans.

Brown McCracken, Janet. 1993. *Valuing diversity: The primary years*. Washington, D.C. NAEYC.

Boutte, Gloria S. (2002). *Resounding voices: School experiences of people from diverse ethnic backgrounds*. Boston, MA: Allyn & Bacon.

Cary, Steven. (1997). *Second language learners*. York, ME: Stenhouse.

Cushner, Kenneth. (2003). *Human diversity in action: An integrative approach*. Boston, MA: McGraw Hill.

Davidman, Leonard. & Davidman, Patricia.T. 2001. *Teaching with a multicultural perspective* (third edition). NY: Longman.

Diaz, Carlos. (2001). *Multicultural education for the 21st century*. NY: Longman.

Echevarria, Jana. & Graves, Anne. (1998). *Sheltered content instruction*. Boston, MA: Allyn & Bacon.

Freire, Paolo. (2000). *Education for critical consciousness*. NY: Continuum

Gay, Geneva. (1994). *At the essence of learning*. Multicultural Education. IN: Kappa Delta Pi.

Giroux, Henry. & McLaren, Peter.(1994). *Between borders: Pedagogy and the politics of cultural studies*. NY: Routledge.

Giroux, Henry. (1996). *Fugitive cultures: Race, violence and youth*. NY: Routledge.

Grant, Carl& Sleeter, Christine. (1993). *Making choices for multicultural education*. New York: Merrill.

Gonzalez, Juan L. (1990). *Racial and ethnic groups in America*. (3d. Edition). Dubuque, IO: Kendall/Hunt Publishing Company.

Gorski, Paul. C. (2001). *Multicultural education and the Internet: Intersections and integrations*. NY: McGraw Hill.

Hernandez, Hilda. (2001). *Multicultural education: A teacher's guide to linking context, process and content*. (2nd Edition). NJ: Merrill/Prentice Hall.

Hoge, John D. (1996). *Effective elementary social studies*. Boston: Wadsworth Publishing Co.

Johnson, David W., Johnson, Roger T., & Holubec, Edythe J. (1994). *The new circles of learning*. Alexandria, VA.: ASCD.

Kamii, Constance. (Ed.) (1990). *Achievement testing in the early grades: The games people play*. Washington DC.: NAEYC.

Kuzmeskus, James. (Ed.) (1996). *We teach them all: Teachers writing about diversity*. York ,ME: Stenhouse.

Loewen, James W. (1995). *Lies my teacher told me*. NY: Simon & Schuster.

Manning, M.Lee & Baruth, Leroy G. (2004). *Multicultural education for children and adolescents*. (fourth edition). NY: Pearson.

McLaren, Peter. (2003). *Life in schools*. (fourth edition). NY: Allyn & Bacon.

Nieto, Sonia. (2000). *Affirming diversity: The sociopolitical context of multicultural education*. NY: Longman.

Ooka Pang, Valerie. (2001). *Multicultural education: A caring-centered approach*. NY: McGraw Hill.

Ovando, Carlos J., Collier, Virginia P., & Combs, Mary C. (2003*). Bilingual ESL classrooms: Teaching in multicultural contexts*. NY: McGraw Hill.

Paley, Vivian. (1984). *Boys and girls.* Chicago, IL: University of Chicago Press.

Sleeter, Christine.E. & Grant, Carl A. (1993). *Making choices for multicultural education* (second edition). NY: McMillan Publishing Company.

Tiedt, Pamela. L. & Tiedt, Iris M. (2002). *Multicultural teaching: A handbook of activities information and resources* (sixth edition). Boston, MA: Allyn & Bacon.

Ukpokodu, Omniota. (1999). *Multiculturalism and globalism*. Social Education. pp. 298–300.

Valle, R. (1997). *Ethnic diversity and multiculturalism: Crisis or challenge*. NY: American Heritage Custom Publishing.

Villegas, A. (1991). *Culturally responsive pedagogy for the1990s and beyond*. Princeton, NJ: Educational Testing.

Zaslavsky, C. (1996). *The multicultural math classroom*. Portsmouth, NH: Heineman.

Index